THE

ACCLES MACHINE GUN

(PATENTED)

CARRIAGES & MOUNTS

The Naval & Military Press Ltd

The Naval & Military Press Ltd
Unit 10 Ridgewood Industrial Park,
Uckfield, East Sussex,
TN22 5QE England
Tel: +44 (0) 1825 749494
Fax: +44 (0) 1825 765701
www.naval-military-press.com

In reprinting in facsimile from the original, any imperfections are inevitably reproduced and the quality may fall short of modern type and cartographic standards.

THE ACCLES MACHINE GUN.

The ACCLES MACHINE GUN is a modification and improvement of the Gatling type of Machine Gun.

Vibration. Among the many improvements that have been effected is the important one that the shaft of the lever which actuates the gun is concentric with the trunnions, and thus all vibration, which tends to destroy accuracy of fire, is avoided when the gun is being rapidly worked. By a simple clutch at the side, the firing mechanism can be thrown in or out of gear instantaneously, and consequently the gunner can either throw a continuous stream of bullets, or fire shot by shot, the handle being turned at a steady rate all the time.

Mountings. The guns are mounted on Field Carriages, Parapet and Embrasure Mountings, and on Naval Mountings. In the latter case they are arranged to be actuated both by hand and by electricity, the main current from the ship's dynamo being led to a small motor which is connected with the shaft which works the gun. *Rapidity of Fire.* Great rapidity of fire is obtained with this arrangement, 1,000 shots per minute having been fired with the electro-motor. By the application of this motor two men can effectively operate the gun, one to point and fire, the other to supply the ammunition.

Barrels. The advantage of having several barrels in a machine gun instead of only one, where rapidity of fire with the new small calibres and smokeless powders is demanded, is daily becoming more evident, and in the ACCLES gun are to be found all the best features which the experience of the last few years has shown to be indispensible.

Feed. The measure of the practical efficiency of a Machine Gun, whether automatic in its action or not, resides in the method of supply of its ammunition :—In other words in the "Feed." This is well known to be the case, and has long proved the chief difficulty with most of the existing Machine Guns.

Ammunition supply.

Not only should the mechanism for the supply of the cartridges to the gun be simple, positive and exact in its action, but the arrangements adopted for insuring a continuous and renewed supply should be equally simple and effective.

Supply of Ammunition.

The only complete solution of the question is in devising a system by which all accessory re-charging of bands, hoppers, or drums is entirely dispensed with, and by which the ammunition, *as transported and carried on to the field, is taken direct from the boxes in which it is packed and carried, and inserted at once into the gun without any preparatory arrangements whatever.*

This important advantage is entirely secured by the new feed device invented by Mr. J. G. ACCLES.

Feed boxes.

The cartridges are packed in the usual ammunition boxes, such as are everywhere used for the storage and transport of ammunition. Instead of being made up in packets and tied with string, the cartridges, twenty in number, are packed flat in a cardboard case lying on a thin continuous strip of tin. Made up in this manner, the cases of cartridges pack very closely and compactly into the ammunition box, and are thoroughly protected against jolting. The ammunition boxes are brought to the gun, opened, the cartridge packets taken out, the folding paper cover striped off, and the packets inserted at once into the gun.

Feeding.

Feeder.

The feeding mechanism is so devised that it at once seizes the first cartridge contained in the fluted tin strip, and forces, *by an absolutely positive action*, the contained cartridges successively into the gun, discharging the tin strip at the other side.

Rate of fire.

The rate of feed of ammunition depends entirely on the speed with which the cartridge packets can be inserted, which is far beyond the probable requirements of firing. Speeds at the rate of 800 to 1,000 rounds per minute have been maintained without difficulty.

Simplicity and Efficiency.

The simplicity and efficiency of this new invention leaves nothing to be desired. Its advantages in respect of saving of time, trouble, and men in action, and in simplifying the service of the gun, and rendering it absolutely reliable by abolishing many complicated devices and operations, are such as to constitute a most important new departure in the use of this class of weapons.

CLAIMS MADE FOR THE ACCLES MACHINE GUN.

1st.—The construction of the Gun is such that it is impossible for an accident to happen to any of the Gunners, through any accidental explosion in the mechanism of the Gun, caused by damaged or imperfect ammunition. The cartridges are received on one side, and are carried round and fired on the opposite side of the Gun, so that its diameter is between the firing point and the feed port. As the rear end of the lock runs in grooves cut in a cam, they are always supported and backed up, and therefore cannot possibly be blown out at any part of their movement. *Complete safety.*

2nd.—As the Gun fires only one shot at a time, the force of the discharge is absorbed by the weight of the Gun, so that there is no recoil or disarrangement of the aim caused by the firing. *Accuracy.*

3rd.—With the crank at the rear, a ten Barrel Gun will fire ten shots for each turn of the crank, or thirty shots a second, which is at the rate of 1,800 shots per minute. *Rapidity.*

4th.—All the movements of the Gun are absolutely positive, certain, and accurate; nothing is left to gravity or chance. *Positive action.*

5th.—As the firing is divided among a number of barrels, they are less subject to heating than Guns of one or two barrels. At no time has it been found necessary to provide them with a water jacket. *Heating.*

Endurance. 6th.—The Gun is designed and built to withstand rough usage neccessary for field service. Damage to one or more barrels or locks will not put the Gun out of action. The Gun can go on firing as long as there is a complete lock and barrel left in it.

Aiming. 7th.—For firing at moving objects, the Gun is arranged to be pointed by means of a shoulder rest or lever, and fired with a trigger. For close sighting at stationary objects, fine adjustment is provided.

Weight. 8th.—The weight depends upon the number of barrels, and the service for which it is intended. The weight varies from 70 to 250 lbs.

Simplicity. 9th.—In estimating the simplicity of the Accles Gun in comparison with other Machine Guns, the number of barrels should be taken into account; it will be found that the Accles Gun has fewer pieces, and is more simple—barrel for barrel—than any other machine Gun in existence.

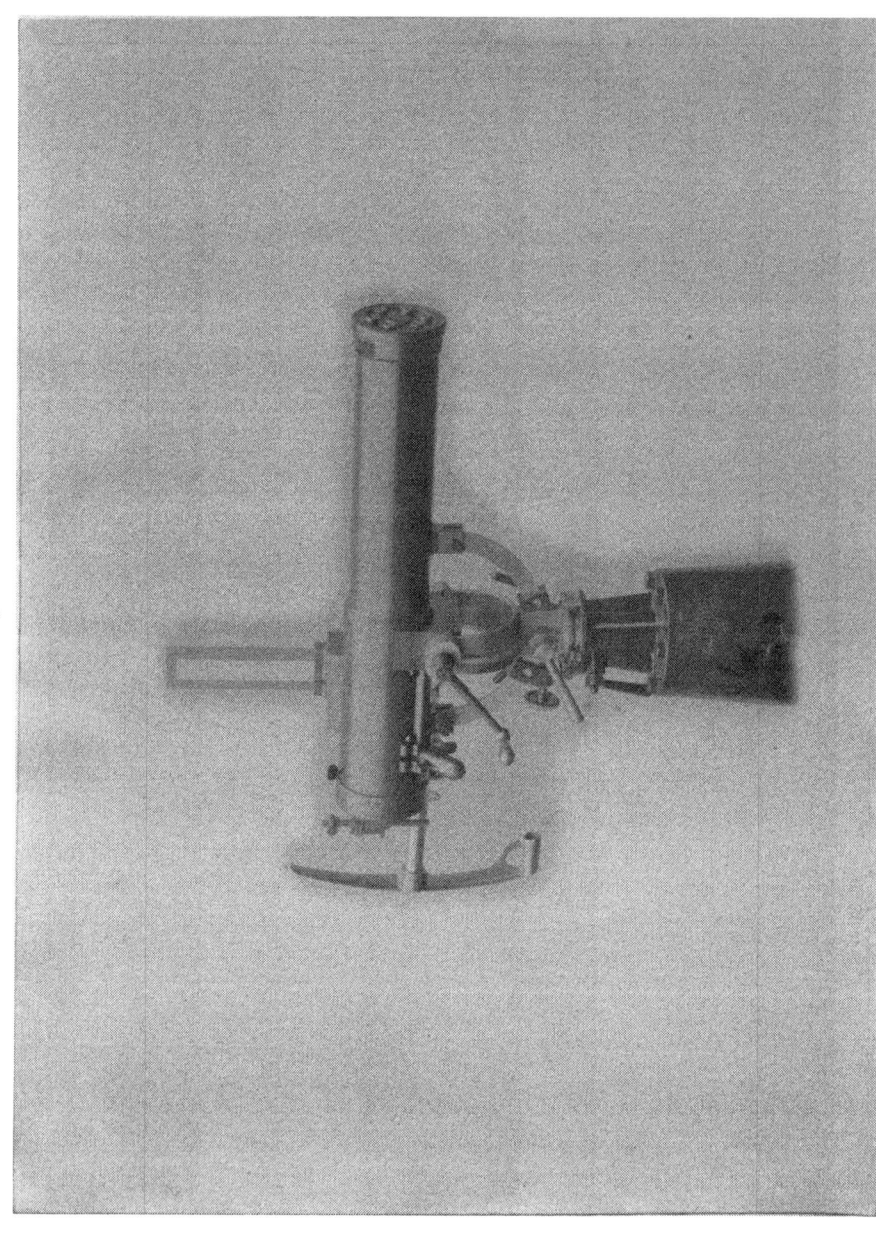

DESCRIPTION OF THE GUN.

THE Gun has 5, 6, 8, or 10 barrels (18)*, and weighs from 70 to 250-lbs. The barrels are grouped around a central spindle (17) which revolves inside the gun case (2). Each barrel has its corresponding lock (23). When the gun is in operation the locks and barrels revolve together. In addition to revolving, the locks are given a forward and backward motion by inclined grooves in a cam (5), which is fixed at the rear end of the gun case. This cam is divided into four parts, viz.: Cam.

    1st. The receiving.
    2nd. The loading.
    3rd. The firing.
    4th. The extracting.

The first part of the cam, which is flat, keeps the lock back until the cartridge has passed from the feeder (9) or cartridge box into the receiver (8) groove in front of the lock.

The second part is an inclined groove along which the locks are forced, thus pushing the cartridges forward into the barrels. About two-thirds along this groove the firing pin (23A), which is contained in the lock, and projects to the rear, comes in contact with the cocking device (5E), and is held back while the lock is carried forward. When the lock arrives at the end of the groove, it passes on to the firing surface (5A), the third part of the cam. At this point, the cartridge is forced tightly into the barrel, and is supported by the lock abutting on the firing surface. The firing pin, which is drawn back, slips off the cocking device and fires the cartridge. Loading.
Firing surface.
Firing.

The firing surface is flat, so the cartridges are held tightly in the chamber during one-fourth of the revolution of the gun,

* The Figures in Brackets refer to the Drawings.
See Plates I and II.

Hang fire.	thus giving a good long dwell in case a cartridge should hang fire. (This firing surface is made of steel, hardened.) As each lock arrives at the end of the firing surface, it passes
Extracting.	into the extracting groove of the cam (the fourth part), which draws the lock to the rear, and with it the empty cartridge case, which is drawn out of the barrel by the extractor (23F), contained in the front part of the lock. When the lock arrives at the end of the extracting groove, it returns into the first part of the cam, which is the receiving part. The empty case, which has been drawn back with the lock along the
Ejecting.	receiver groove, comes in contact with two curved ejector points (9N) which dip down into two circular grooves cut into the receiver, the points thus passing under the case and rolling it out of the receiver grooves and ejecting it from the gun. In the meantime, the empty receiver groove has passed on and received another cartridge from the feeder or cartridge box, and the operation of loading, firing, and ejecting the empty shell is repeated.
Loading.	Thus as the gun is turned, each lock, as it passes in front of the feeder mouth, receives a cartridge, passes it through the operation of loading, firing and ejecting the empty case from the gun. When firing, five cartridges are in the various stages of loading, firing and extracting. Although the gun can be
Rapidity.	fired up to 1000 shots per minute, only one shot is fired at a
Recoil.	time, so the recoil of the gun is only equal to the force of one discharge, and is taken up in the weight of the gun, so there is little or no movement while firing which would tend to dis-arrange the aim. The backward force of each discharge is taken up through the lock on the firing surface of the cam, which is fixed at the rear end of the gun case, and held in its place by the breech-plate, which is screwed and locked on to the case in such a manner that it cannot possibly move.
Forward force.	The forward movement of the barrels, caused by the discharge, is taken up by a steel check disc (12) connected to the main spindle and barrels about three inches in front of the rear end of the barrels; this presses against a shoulder or step cut around the inside of the case in front of the trunnions, thus holding the barrels and locks so firmly between the shoulder on the case and the firing surface of the cam, that

it is not possible for any "give" or spring to take place on the head of the cartridge at the time of discharge. Rigidity of gun

The lock is made of a straight piece of steel, arranged at the rear end to fit the grooves of the cam, and is provided with a T projection on the under side to guide and hold it in its proper place as it moves forward and backward along the T grooves in the guide cylinder and receiver. Locks.

The firing pin is a piece of round steel running through the centre of the lock, with a flanged head (to catch on to the cocking device) and projecting at the rear end. The striking force of the firing pin is given by a spiral spring (23E) which is held in the lock by a screwed bush (23c) at the rear end: at the front end of the spring, sliding on the firing pin, is a small bush (23B) which is drawn back with the spring by the firing pin until the spring is compressed. When the firing pin slips off the cocking device, the spring forces the small bush and firing pin forward; just before the full stroke of the firing pin is completed the small bush is stopped by a shoulder in the lock. The firing pin continues moving forward until stopped by the cap or the second shoulder in the lock. The firing pin is by this means left free to move back after striking the cap, so that the point does not project and allow any chance of a premature explosion while pushing the cartridge forward into the barrel. Firing pin.
Spring.
Rebound.

The extractor is fitted to the underside of the lock partly in the T way, and has a slight backward and forward movement. The rear end of the extractor is round, and fits into a small hole in the T part of the lock. The front end of the extractor is provided with a small wedge-shaped projection which notches into a similarly formed notch in the front end of the lock. The object of this is to draw the extractor, by means of the wedge, tight against the head of the cartridge as the lock moves to the rear. The underpart of the extractor is also bevelled. When the gun is in operation, the extractor slides along the bottom of the T groove in the receiver until it comes to a narrow part near the front end, at which point the bottom of the groove is deeper, so that the extractor can slip down and pass over the head or rim of the cartridge, should it have got in front of the extractor hook while loading. Extractor.

When the lock is drawn to the rear after firing, the underpart of the extractor comes against an incline (7) arranged in the bottom of the narrow groove of the receiver and forces the extractor up against the cartridge head; thus giving the extractor a positive grip on the head of the cartridge case.

To remove locks. The locks are inserted and removed from the gun through a small hole in the breech plate, which is closed by a round plug or lock port door, (4A) This door is opened by giving it a quarter turn to the right.

Safety cam. The gun is provided with a safety cam (20), which moves back the cocking device out of action so that the firing pins do not come in contact with it while the gun is being operated, and this prevents any undue snapping of the firing pins while the gun is being worked for drill or explanation without firing.

This safety cam is put in and out of action with a key (20A). After many years of experience with machine guns, it has been proved many times that a safety arrangement on a machine gun is a very dangerous attachment if it is so arranged that any person can put it in or out of action at will. As it is necessary to put the gun through all its movements in order *Drill.* to drill the men in its use, it is necessary to provide the gun with means to put the mechanism in and out of action. So to make it as safe as possible, it is arranged to be done with a key. By this means, no one can tamper with the gun, except the men who have keys, and whose duty it would be to see that the gun was in proper order or condition for drill or fire, as required. The gun should never be operated when the cocking device is set for firing, unless cartridges are being fed into the *Snapping of firing pins.* gun. A continual snapping of the firing pins will crystallize the metal and cause the points to drop off. This will happen with all guns used in this way.

Crank. The gun is operated by means of a crank (19). It can be fired with the crank either at the side or at the rear; when placed at the rear six shots are fired at each turn, or as many shots as there are barrels in the gun; and when placed at the side, two *Slow and rapid fire.* shots at each turn. The crank should only be used at the rear when it is necessary to pour a very rapid fire into a given point, as the gun cannot be sighted while the crank is being turned at the rear.

For firing at moving objects, or where the fire requires to be changed from place to place, the crank is placed at the side of the gun and the movement is carried through the trunnion arms, and operated by a worm (13A) and worm-wheel (13). The worm runs free on the worm shaft (13B), and a small clutch ring (21J) is arranged to slide on keys along the shaft and engage with teeth cut on the end of the worm. The clutch ring is moved by a switch (21I), which is operated from the rear end of the gun by a trigger (21).

Pointing.

Trigger.

When in action, one man turns the crank, another man (the pointer) keeps his right hand on the trigger handle (21A) and points the gun by means of the pointing lever or shoulder piece (22) with his left hand. When the gun is on the mark, the pointer presses the trigger which switches the clutch into gear with the worm, and fires the gun; by this arrangement the gun is only fired at the will of the pointer, although the man at the crank keeps turning continually, whether the gun is firing or not.

Firing and Pointing.

By transmitting the motive power through the trunnion arms, which is the dead centre of the gun, there is no shaking or jarring motion given to the gun by the turning of the crank, as is the case with all other guns fired by a crank or lever.

Jarring.

If required, the trigger can be pressed down and left, and the gun will then go on firing as long as the crank is turned.

Continuous firing.

The cartridges are supplied to the gun in paper boxes, holding from ten to twenty-five cartridges each, as found most suitable for transport packing. These boxes are made at the Factory with the cartridges, and filled ready for use direct into the gun. The boxes are made of light cardboard, open at one end and wide enough to take a row of cartridges. On one side are glued two thin strips of cardboard, between which runs a strip of fluted tin about one inch wide; when the box is full, a cartridge lies in each groove of the tin strip, which keeps the cartridges an equal distance apart and in line. The end is sealed up and made air tight by a paper cover arranged with a piece of cloth, so that it can be quickly torn off before placing the box in the feeding mechanism of the gun. To prevent the cartridges from

Supply of ammunition.

Feed box.

dropping out when the cover is torn off, a narrow piece of strong paper is pasted across each end of the opening.

Feeder.

The cartridges are fed into the gun through the feeder (9), which is placed on the left hand side of the gun, and held in its place by two cheeks, cast on the gun case. At the top of the feeder is a narrow opening, into which the paper cartridge box is placed, open side down. At the bottom of the opening are two small wheels (9A), with projecting teeth, into which the first cartridge at the end of the box enters, and at the same moment the body of the cartridge presses down a small lever, (9L) which moves a clutch (9H) into gear with the driving wheel (9K), which is continually driven round by the turning of the gun, and so puts the two feeding wheels into action, drawing the cartridges out of the paper boxes by means of the fluted tin strip, and bringing each cartridge evenly into line with the teeth of the feeding wheels. The cartridges are carried round, out of the tin strips, in a groove on each side of the feeder, and forced into the grooves in the cartridge receiver of the gun. The tin strips pass through the feeder and drop on to the ground, and the empty box is ejected from the feeder by the ejector on the hopper cover.

The two feeding wheels of the feeder do not revolve or turn until a cartridge has been placed in their teeth, and the small lever pressed down, pushing the clutch into gear, where it remains until the last cartridge has passed out of the feed wheels, at which moment the lever flies up, throwing the clutch out of action, and stopping the two wheels. The object of this is to ensure the cartridges being in their proper position before the mechanism is put in motion, thus doing away with any chance of a jam during feeding.

Positive Action of Gun.

It will be seen that, through the whole action of the gun, all the movements are positive; nothing is left to chance or gravity, which is the great defect in all other machine guns. Too much stress cannot be put on the great benefit that is gained by being able to pack the ammunition at the factory in such a way that it can be fed from the box into the gun by a positive movement without re-arranging. This system not only offers the advantage of a positive feed, but admits of a larger quantity of ammunition being carried, than by any other system used with a machine gun, and, when in use, at no time are the cartridges exposed to damp or dust.

Carriage of ammunition

Damage to one or more barrels or locks will not put the gun out of action, as the lock connected with the damaged barrel can be removed and the firing continued. The gun can go on firing as long as there is a good lock and barrel left in it.

Out of action.

The speed of the firing of the gun has been reduced to fire only two shots to one turn of the crank when placed on the side, as it has been found that the speed of 400 shots per minute is quite fast enough for regular service, and especially with the new small bore cartridges using metal covered bullets. The heating power of 1000 shots, fired with small bore ammunition, is equal to 4000 rounds of ammunition with lead bullets. When a moment arrives where a large number of shots are required, the crank can be changed to the rear, which will give a speed of 1000 shots per minute.

No. of shots per minute.

Heating.

The gun can be fired at all degrees of elevation and depression.

Angle of fire

The gun is sighted on the top a little to the right of the centre. The front sight (24I) is made of a piece of round steel coned to a point. The rear sight (24) is a straight steel bar with a sliding leaf (24A) at the top, moved by a screw (24B), and divided into tenths of an inch. The leaf is **V** notched for fine sighting, and has two uprights about $\frac{1}{4}$ of an inch apart, for quick sighting when the gun is firing at moving objects, either on land or sea.

Sights.

The gun is mounted on a **Y** mount, (25)* the arms of which take the trunnions of the gun, which are held in place by caps (25H) locked down with pins (25I) Through the centre of the fork is carried an arc (25A), the two ends of which enter lugs cast on the gun case, and are held in place by arc pins (2C). On one side of the fork is a binding handle (25K) to clamp the arc.

Mount.

On the arc are two stops (25B &C) with binding screws. These stops can be set at any position on the arc to give a vertical oscillation over a given range. The rear stop is fitted

Spread of shot.

* See plate III.

with a screw (25D), by means of which the gun can be given fine adjustment when taking accurate and deliberate aim. The mount ends in a long round stem which can be easily fitted to any form of socket. When required, a shield is fitted to the mount.

This mount has the advantage of being simple and strong, and very suitable for a machine gun, as it has an all-round free movement when pointed with the lever or shoulder rest, and can be given fine adjustment, or locked tight in a moment.

For use at sea, the guns should be fitted with shields, and made with a muzzle preponderance of from 6 to 10 pounds, as the pointer can bring the gun more easily into the line of sight by bearing down on the pointing lever than he can by lifting up.

Electro-motor. For ships' use, in addition to the crank, the gun can be fitted with a small electro-motor attached to the worm shaft and driven from the main current of the ship's dynamo. By this means, two men can easily work the gun; one to point and fire, the other to supply the ammunition to the gun.

To mount the gun in different parts of the ship, various Brackets, Sockets and Pedestals are required, which can only be determined when the position for the gun has been fixed.

Top mount. For mounting the gun on ships' tops special mountings have been designed. They are so arranged that the gun can be moved around the mast on the rail of the top, and the gun can be pointed down so as to drop the shot on to the deck, or close to the side of the ship. The wires from the ship's dynamo can be carried up the mast to work the gun. Special feed boxes can be made (of tin) to hold 50 cartridges. By this arrangement, *one* man could load, fire and point the gun at the rate of 600 shots per minute.

NAVAL LANDING CARRIAGE.—PLATE XV.

The carriage for hand draught, or naval landing service, is made of Steel, and fitted with four ammunition cases, holding 1000 rounds of small bore ammunition each.

Close to the axle, between the two trail cheeks, is fitted a socket, into which the stem of the gun-mount fits. On top of the socket, two plates are arranged so that they can be set to limit the horizontal oscillation of the gun to any required distance or spread. A set of entrenching tools is carried. The spare parts and tools are carried in a small box fitted in the trail. Drag ropes and pulling belts are also provided.

The trail is provided with a moveable cross bar, so that two men can guide the gun while on the move. The carriage is well balanced, and runs lightly. The gun is fired from the carriage without removing the ammunition boxes, and is ready to fire as soon as the trail touches the ground.

Landing party

The landing party should consist of not less than 1 officer and 10 men. Each man should have his rifle. This would give 3 men on each drag rope, 2 at the cross bar of the trail, and two men extra to give a hand at the wheels over rough ground. At the firing position, the arrangement would be, one man at the crank, one man to feed, one man to point and one man to stand by to relieve any of the other operators in case of accident. The other six men would be using their rifles, and thus each man would be engaged.

The carriage is so arranged that it can be quickly taken to pieces and packed away when on board ship, and the carriage ammunition cases placed in the magazine.

Night service.

For night work, if defending a given point, the gun can be set in the day time, and arranged to cover any required space. For instance, if it is necessary to cover a bridge (or landing) and part of the approach, say a space of 200 yards in length, at a distance of 1000 yards, the gun would be put into position while there was daylight, and aimed for 1000 yards, which would be the approximate centre of the bridge. The stops on the arc would then be set and clamped so that the gun would elevate to 1150 yards and depress to 850. This would give a vertical oscillating movement, which would cover 300 yards. The gun would also be given a slight horizontal movement.

The gun is now ready for action. We will suppose that the alarm is given that the enemy is crossing the bridge; the gun would commence firing; the pointer would move the gun up and down between the stops while firing, which would cover the bridge with a stream of bullets. As a rapid fire would be more effectual, the gun would be fired with the crank at the rear.

For street defence this gun has no equal. By setting the stops on the arc, the gun could be given a vertical oscillation that would take in the whole length of the street, or up to the extreme range of the gun.

Weight. The greater the weight the greater the accuracy and uniformity of fire. The weight of the gun should be consistent with its portability and accuracy; *i.e.* the weight should not be so great as to prevent its being lifted and moved by two men; at the same time it should be heavy enough to take up the recoil of each discharge.

After long experience and repeated trials it has been demonstrated that the most suitable weight for a practical machine gun, for service on land and sea, is about 150 lbs., exclusive of carriage and mounts.

This weight can easily be handled by two men, and is sufficient to take up the recoil.

While guns of lighter weight—90 to 100 lbs.—will do good service, they will, of course, not have the same stability as a heavier one, as the "jump" due to the recoil will more or less interfere with the accuracy during rapid fire.

All of this will, of course, depend on the ammunition used, and the amount of recoil from the explosion.

These conclusions have been arrived at from experiments with black powder. No doubt smokeless powder, having a less recoil, would admit of a lighter gun to give the same stability. But inasmuch as the use of smokeless powders in machine guns is to a great extent in the experimental stage, it has not been deemed advisable to reduce the weight of the standard machine guns at present.

And in building guns for general service on land and sea, the weight has been kept as near 150 lbs. as possible; but of course the weight will vary somewhat with the calibre and service charge of the ammunition to be used.

But for special service where lightness is a great desideratum, particularly when the modern small bore service ammunition is to be used, it is believed that guns built to a weight of 70 to 100 lbs. would give eminent satisfaction, and would combine great endurance of working parts with ease of manipulation and high accuracy of fire.

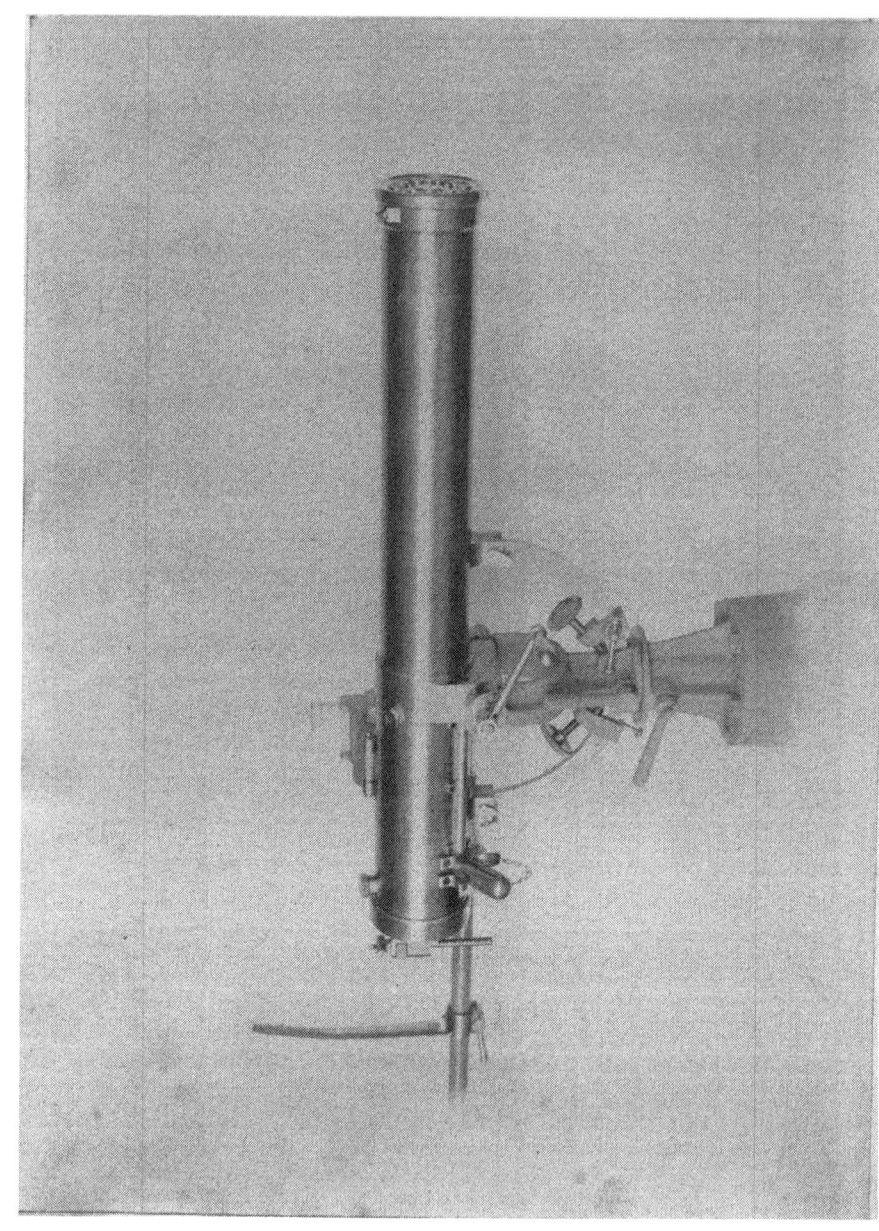

WEIGHTS AND DIMENSIONS

OF THE

ACCLES MACHINE GUN.

	6 BARREL	10 BARREL
CALIBRE	·303in.	·303in.
NUMBER OF BARRELS	6	10
TOTAL LENGTH OF GUN	41·5in.	43·5in.
DIAMETER OF GUN AT BREECH	6·75 ,,	6·75 ,,
,, ,, ,, MUZZLE	6·25 ,,	6.25 ,,
LENGTH OF BARREL	28 ,,	30 ,,
,, ,, RIFLING	25·7 ,,	27·7 ,,
NUMBER OF GROOVES	7	7
DEPTH OF GROOVES	·004in.	·004in.
TWIST OF RIFLING, ONE TURN IN	10in.	10in.
SYSTEM OF RIFLING	Metford	Metford
CHAMBER TO TAKE	Mag. ·303in. (English)	Mag. ·303in. (English)
DIAMETER OF BARREL AT BREECH	$1\frac{1}{8}$in.	$1\frac{1}{8}$in.
WEIGHT OF BARREL	5 lbs.	$5\frac{1}{4}$lbs.
,, GUN COMPLETE	150 lbs.	220lbs.
,, Y MOUNT	26 lbs.	26 ,,
ELEVATION EXTREME	50 deg.	50 deg.
DEPRESSION EXTREME	50 ,,	50 ,,
RATE OF FIRE PER MINUTE, CRANK AT SIDE	360	500
,, ,, ,, ,, ,, REAR	700	1200
AMMUNITION, KIND	Eng: Service ·303in.	Eng: Service ·303in.
TOTAL LENGTH OF CARTRIDGE	3in.	3in.
,, ,, OF CASE	2·2 ,,	2·2 ,,
,, ,, OF BULLET	1·25 ,,	1·25 ,,
KIND OF BULLET	N'kel Covered	N'kel covered
WEIGHT OF BULLET	215 grs.	215 grs.
CHARGE OF POWDER	70 ,,	70 ,,
KIND OF POWDER	Pellet.	Pellet
RANGE, EXTREME		

NOTE.—*This table alters with guns of different calibre.*

LIST OF PARTS OF THE GUN.
—— PLATE I. ——

Fig. 1. **Gun complete.**

„ 2. **Gun case.**
„ 2A. Cover for trunnion box.
„ 2B. Spring.
„ 2C. Arc pins.
„ 2D. Stop screws.

„ 3. **Rear nut.**
„ 3A. Taper pin.

„ 4. **Breech plate.**
„ 4A. Lock port door.
* „ 4B. Friction pin.
* „ 4C. Stop screw.
„ 4D. Chain eye.
„ 4E. Chain and ring.
„ 4F. Sight bracket.
* „ 4G. „ „ screws.
* „ 4H. „ „ springs.
* „ 4I. „ „ „ screws.

„ 5. **Cam.**
* „ 5A. Firing surface.
* „ 5B. „ „ screws.
* „ 5C. Key.
* „ 5D. „ screw.
„ 5E. Cocking device
„ 5F. „ „ pin
„ 5G. „ „ spring
„ 5H. „ „ stop plate

„ 6. **Friction ring, centre of case.**

Fig. 7. **Extractor ring.**

„ 8. **Receiver and Lock cylinder.**
„ 8A. Feeder driving ring
„ 8B. „ „ pins.
* „ 8C. „ „ screws.

„ 9. **Feeder.**
„ 9A. „ wheels
„ 9B. „ „ gear.
„ 9C. „ „ spindle.
* „ 9D. „ „ pins.
„ 9E. Centre gear.
* „ 9F. „ „ spindle.
„ 9G. Clutch gear.
„ 9H. Clutch.
„ 9I. „ spindle.
* „ 9J. „ spring.
„ 9K. Driving wheel.
„ 9L. Starting lever & spring.
„ 9M. Holding lever.
„ 9N. Ejector points.
* „ 9P. Screws.
* „ 9Q. Wheel box cover.
* „ 9R. Case screws.
„ 9S. Cover.
„ 9T. Box ejector.
„ 9V. „ „ spring.
„ 9X. „ „ pin & plug.
* „ 9Y. Locking Pin.

„ 10. **Shell guide.**

„ 11. **Disc for locking barrels.**

° *Not shewn in drawing.*

LIST OF PARTS OF THE GUN, Continued.

Fig. 12.	**Check disc for stopping barrels.**	
,, 12A.	Barrel bush.	
,, 13.	**Driving or worm wheel.**	
,, 13A.	Worm.	
,, 13B.	,, shaft.	
,, 13C.	,, ,, ferrule.	
,, 13D.	,, ,, taper pin.	
,, 14.	**Front disc.**	
,, 14A.	Taper pin.	
,, 14B.	Support ring.	
,, 15.	**Friction ring, front.**	
,, 16.	**Dust ring.**	
,, 16A.	,, binding screw.	
,, 17.	**Main spindle.**	
,, 17A.	Binding nut.	
*,, 17B.	Taper pin.	
,, 17C.	Friction ring (rear).	
,, 18.	**Barrels.**	
,, 19.	**Crank.**	
,, 19A.	Handle.	
,, 19B.	Catch pin.	
,, 20.	**Safety cam.**	
*,, 20A.	,, key.	
,, 21.	**Trigger.**	
,, 21A.	,, handle.	
*,, 21B.	,, taper pin.	
*,, 21C.	,, spring.	
*,, 21D.	,, pins.	
*,, 21E.	,, nut.	
,, 21F.	Shaft.	
,, 21G.	Shaft cover.	
,, 21H.	Shaft cover screws.	

Fig. 21I.	Switch.	
,, 21J.	Clutch.	
*,, 22	**Pointing lever.**	
*,, 22A.	,, ,, arm.	
*,, 22B.	,, ,, pins.	
,, 23.	**Locks.**	
,, 23A.	Firing pin.	
,, 23B.	Stop nut, or brush.	
,, 23C.	Screw bush.	
*,, 23D.	Binding screw.	
,, 23E.	Spring.	
,, 23F.	Extractor.	
,, 24.	**Sight bar.**	
,, 24A.	,, leaf.	
*,, 24B.	,, traversing screw.	
,, 24C.	,, nut.	
*,, 24D.	,, ,, taper pin.	
,, 24E.	Elevating nut.	
*,, 24F.	Guide piece.	
*,, 24G.	Friction bar.	
*,, 24H.	Spring.	
*,, 24I.	Front sight.	
*,, 24J.	,, binding screw.	
*,, 24K.	,, oil hole cover.	
,, 25.	**Y Mount.**	
,, 25A.	,, arc.	
,, 25B.	Front stop.	
,, 25C.	Rear stop.	
,, 25D.	,, adjusting screw.	
,, 25E.	Friction nut.	
,, 25F.	,, spring.	
,, 25G.	Friction shoe.	
,, 25H.	Trunnion caps.	
,, 25I.	,, pins.	
,, 25J.	,, screws.	
,, 25K.	Binding handle.	

* *Not shewn in drawing.*

TOOLS AND SPARE PARTS.

The following is a list of tools and spare parts supplied with each gun:—

TOOLS.

1 Brass cleaning rod.
1 Screw driver.
1 ,, ,, for locks.
1 ,, ,, for binding nut.
1 Shifting spanner.
1 Large steel pin punch.
2 Small ,, ,, punches.
1 Oil can.
1 Tallow box.
1 Barrel plug, brass
1 Rear plug.
1 Shell ejector.
3 Safety cam keys.

SPARE PARTS.

1 Lock complete.
3 ,, firing pins.
2 ,, stop nuts.
2 ,, screw bushes.
3 ,, bush screws.
3 ,, springs.
3 ,, extractors.
3 Springs for cocking device.
1 Large taper pin.
2 Small taper pins.
6 ,, screws, various.

GENERAL INSTRUCTIONS.

DIRECTIONS FOR TAKING THE GUN TO PIECES.

Place the Gun horizontally on a bench or its own mounting. 1st Position.

When on its own mounting, see that all the clamps are tight, or the front end of the gun will drop and damage the case when the rear parts are removed. Note.

To remove the locks (23) turn the lock port door (4A) to the right and draw it to the rear. Turn the gun backwards with the crank (19) until the lock comes in line with the opening; then draw the lock out by hand. Repeat the operation until all the locks are removed. 2nd Locks.

Knock out the taper pin (3A) and draw off the rear nut (3). 3rd Rear nut.

To remove the rear sight bar (24), give it a half turn and draw it out. 4th Sight.

Take out the screw (4C) and turn the Breech-plate (4) to the left, and unscrew. 5th Breech-plate.

Draw the Cam (5) to the rear (by hand) out of the case (2). 6th Cam.

Take care that the small round safety cam (20) at the front end of the cocking device (5E) does not drop out and get lost. Note.

Should the Cam (5) stick in the case (2) so that it cannot be drawn out by hand, leave it until the barrels (18) (12th operation) are drawn out, at which time it will come away with them.

To remove the cocking device (5E) press down the small pin (5F) and slide off the cover (5H). Remove the pin (5F) spring (5G) and cocking device (5E). 6th A Cocking device.

To remove, turn up the locking pin (9Y) at the right side of Feeder, then draw the Feeder horizontally away from the gun. 7th Feeder.

Lift it out (10). 8th Shell Guide.

To remove, press the small pin (19B) in the crank shaft away from the spindle (13B) and draw off. 9th Crank.

10th Worm shaft.	To remove, knock out the small taper pin (13D) at the left hand side of the Trunnion box, and draw the shaft (13B) out from the right hand side.
11th Worm and clutch.	Press down the small spring (2B) and pull the slide (2A), which covers the trunnion box, to the rear, and the worm (13A), clutch (21J), and ferrule (13C) will drop out.
12th Barrels.	Draw the barrels and the remaining parts of the gun mechanism to the rear, and out of the case.
13th Dust ring.	Loose the small binding screw (16A) on the under side of the dust ring (16) and turn the ring to the right until it screws off the case. Take out the friction ring (15).
Note.	The thread of the dust ring is left-handed, so that it will tighten up by the turning of the gun.
14th Trigger.	Knock out the small pin (21B) which passes through the trigger shaft (21F), press the trigger shaft to the front and draw it out at the front of the trunnion box, catch the switch (21I) which will drop out of the trunnion box, take out the screws, and remove the trigger handle (21A).
15th Barrels	To dismount, knock out the taper pin (17B) at the rear end of the lock cylinder (8) and remove the binding nut (17A). Take off the lock cylinder (8) and receiver, slightly elevate the front end of the barrels with a piece of wood, and push the main spindle (17) to the front, and with it the front barrel disc (14). Draw the disc for locking the barrels (11) to the rear, and the barrels (18) are free to be taken out.
16th Case.	To remove, turn the two pins (2C), which pass through the two lugs and the ends of the arc, a quarter turn to the rear, and draw two-thirds out, or until stopped by the small screws in the lugs. Turn the two pins (25I) in the trunnion caps (25H) half round and draw away from the gun until stopped. Raise the caps (25H) and remove the case from the mount.
17th Feeder.	To take Feeder to pieces, remove wheel box cover (9Q), lift out the three gears (9B), (9E), (9G); take out the two screws (9R) and lift away the top half off the Feeder. Remove clutch (9H) and spring (9J), lift off starting lever (9L), remove shaft (9C) with feeder wheels (9A) and holding lever (9M), then draw away driving wheel (9K) with its shaft (9I).

To assemble the Feeder, follow the directions for taking the feeder to pieces, but in inverse order. *Assembling feeder.*

In replacing the three gears, take care that their teeth engage opposite the letters **AA** and **BB** on the face of the gears, otherwise the Gun will not be fed properly, as the pitching will be wrong. *Note.*

If the feeder wheels (9A) have been removed from their shaft (9C), see that in replacing them that the letters **C** and **D** on the shaft come opposite the letters **C** and **D** on the wheels.

In replacing the holding lever (9M)—which comes between the two feeder wheels (9A)—see that the letter **E** on its rim coincides with the letter **E** on the hubs of the feeder wheels.

TO ASSEMBLE THE GUN.

Place the case (2) horizontally on a bench or on its own mount. See that the centre friction ring (6) is in position and covered with tallow. *1st Operation case.*

When on its own mount, see that the clamps are tight. *Note.*

Place the friction ring (15) in position. Screw on the dust ring (16) by turning it to the left until the mark on the ring comes in line with the mark on the case (2). Then screw in the small binding screw (16A). *2nd Dust ring.*

The friction ring should be well oiled, and covered with tallow. *Note.*

Screw on the trigger handle (21A) and shaft cover (21G), taking care that the trigger (21) is in its place in the trigger handle. Place the switch (21I) in the trunnion box with the letter " R " to the rear. Pass the trigger shaft (21F) through the trunnion box and switch (21I) from the front until the end of the shaft (21F) enters the trigger (21). Bring the holes in the trigger (21) and shaft in line, and drive in the taper pin (21B). *3rd Trigger.*

Lay the rear barrel disc (11) on a flat surface, and place the barrels (18) in position side by side, slide the barrel bushes (12A) on to the barrels. Put the driving wheel (13) and the stop disc in position (12). Take care that the right side is up, and that the key grooves in the discs (11) are in line. Place *4th Barrels.*

the support ring (14B) on the front end of the barrels (18), and then lay them horizontally on the bench. Place the front disc (14) on the front end of the main spindle (17), and drive in the taper pin (14A), slide the spindle along between the barrels (18) through the centre of the driving wheel (13) and the disc for locking barrels (11), taking care that the key on the spindle is in line with the groove in the discs, and that the front end of the barrels enter the front disc properly. Slide the receiver and cylinder (8) on to the spindle (17) and screw on the binding nut (17A) until the taper hole through the rear end of the cylinder comes in line with the hole in the nut (17A) and spindle, then drive in the taper pin (17B), put on the friction washer (17C) and slide the barrels into the case.

Note. Take care that the friction washer (17C) is not forgotten, and that it is well covered with tallow, also the front barrel disc (14).

5th Shell guide. Place the shell guide (10) in position.

6th Cam. Place the safety cam (20) in position in front of the cocking device (5E), and push the cam into the rear end of the case (2). See that the key in the cam comes in line with the keyway in the case, and push it as far forward as it will go.

Note. The cocking device (5E) should be well oiled, and the projecting part, which engages with the firing pins (23A) should be covered with tallow, also the firing surface (5A) of the cam.

6th A Cocking device. To replace, place the cocking piece (5E.) in the T groove of the cam, put in the spring (5G) and pin (5F), press down the pin and push on the slide (5H) until the spring pin enters the small hole in the slide (5H),

Note. See that the cocking device is well oiled, and that it works freely.

7th Breech-plate. Screw on the breech plate (4) and insert the holding screw (4C).

8th Rear nut. Push on the rear nut (3) and drive in the taper pin (3A).

9th Worm and clutch. Place the clutch (21J) in the clutch teeth of the worm (13A), and lift up into the trunnion box, taking care that the circular groove in the clutch (21J) enters the switch points (21I). When up in line, push the worm shaft (13B) through the trunnions, worm (13A) and clutch (21J); push the worm and clutch to the right, and push the brass ferrule (13C) up to the left of the worm, and push the worm shaft (13B) into place through the ferrule, taking care that the keys on the shaft (13B) enter the grooves on the clutch (21J). Drive in the taper pin (13D) and put on the crank (19).

Note. The worm and clutch should be well oiled in the bearings, and the teeth covered with tallow.

10th Locks. Turn the gun backwards until the T grooves in the cylinder (8) come in line with the lockport " A " and push in the lock (23) and so on until all the locks are in. Put in the lockport door (4A) and turn to the left.

Note. The inside of the locks should be oiled, and the outside covered with tallow. When all the locks are in, the gun should be turned five or six times to see that it works properly.

11th Feeder. Put the feeder (9) into position, taking care that the driving wheel (9K) goes into its proper position in the pin ring (8A).

12th Sight. To remove and replace the tangent sight (24), turn it half round so that the teeth on the bar do not engage with the threads in the nut (24E), and slide it up or down as required. When in the proper position, turn the bar into gear with the nut, and then raise or lower by turning the nut.

13th Lock. To dismount, push the extractor (23F) to the rear out of the bevel cut, and pull it out. Unscrew the small screw (23D) half way, then unscrew the screw bush (23C) and withdraw the firing pin (23A). Compress the spring (23E) until the stop nut (23B) comes opposite the narrow part of the firing pin (23A), and take it off and remove the spring.

To replace, the same directions are followed as for taking to pieces, but in inverse order.

Note.

Care should be taken that all the parts are clean and well oiled when replaced.

CARE AND PRESERVATION OF THE GUN.

The following important points should be carefully attended to just before and after firing :—

> Allow no person to go in front of the gun at any time while the crank is being turned.
>
> Before firing, see that the feeder and shell guide are in place and properly secured.
>
> See that the safety cam is set at "fire," and that the crank is locked to the worm spindle.
>
> Turn the crank slowly, and see that the feeder works smoothly, and that the lock moves freely.
>
> Oil all the working parts of the gun.

When the safety cam is set at "fire," and no cartridges are being fed into the gun do not turn the crank more than is absolutely necessary, as the continual snapping of the firing pins against the inside of the lock will in time crystallize the metal and cause the points to drop off.

AFTER FIRING.

The safety cam should be set at "safe" and the key removed.

Take off the feeder. Turn the crank backwards and see that there are no cartridges or shells left in the gun.

Examine the feeder and see that there are no cartridges left in it.

The mechanism, barrels, chambers and every part of the gun should be kept free from rust, and rubbed with oil or tallow.

If possible, the locks and barrels should be cleaned every morning.

To do this, remove the feeder, withdraw the locks, clean the barrels, and oil very lightly, clean the locks and cover with tallow on the outside, and replace in the gun. Oil the working parts of the feeder, and replace.

The locks and other parts of the gun only require to be taken to pieces for cleaning after firing, or after the gun has been on the march.

When cleaning the gun turpentine or oil is to be used; on no account should emery cloth or any cutting substance be allowed.

JAMMING.

Jamming will be caused by the following defects in the ammunition:—

1st. The cartridge head blowing off and leaving the body of the cartridge case in the chamber of the barrel.

2nd. The cartridge case splitting while firing and leaving a hard deposit of burnt powder in the chamber and receiver.

With due care in the inspection of the cartridges none of these accidents will occur. None but the best and most carefully inspected cartridges should be used.

When the cartridge head blows off and leaves the body of the cartridge case in the chamber, the next cartridge can only partly enter and will stop the gun.

To remove, take off the feeder and turn the gun backwards until the cause of the jam is found. If it should be a head off, and the broken cartridge case does not come out with the one which was forced into it, push the shell ejector into the chamber, with the spring lips towards the front of the gun, and then drive out with the cleaning rod.

Replace the feeder and continue the firing.

Should the chamber and the cartridge receiver become clogged with a deposit from the burnt powder, they should be oiled freely, which will soften the burnt powder.

In case of a lock or barrel becoming disabled, it is essential that the stop plugs be inserted in the chamber and in the hole through which the front end of the lock passes into the receiver; otherwise, cartridges are liable to enter the chamber or lock port hole of the disabled barrel and cause a jam.

DESCRIPTION OF Y MOUNT.

Weight .. .. 26 lbs.

The mount is made of gun metal, with two upright arms, into which the trunnions of the gun fit, and are held in place by two caps (25H), held down by pins (25I). Passing through the centre of the mount is a steel arc (25A), the ends of which fit into lugs on the gun case (2), and are held in place by pins (2C). At the right hand side is a binding screw and handle (25K) for clamping the arc at any desired position. To prevent the gun from moving too freely, or dropping when the clamp is undone, a friction shoe is arranged to act on the arc, by means of the nut (25E) on the left hand side.

By screwing up the nut it acts on a spring (25F) which presses a pin or shoe (25G) against the arc, and puts on the desired amount of tension. The arc is provided with two stops (25B & 25c). The rear stop (25c) is arranged with a screw (25D) which passes through the under part and comes against the mount. This screw is for the purpose of giving fine adjustment to the gun for fine sighting. The lower part of the mount ends in a long round stem, which fits into the various stands and sockets.

TO TAKE THE MOUNT TO PIECES.

Remove the gun, slack off the friction nut (25E) and loose the clamp handle (25K), take off the front stop (25B) and draw away the arc (25A).

TO REPLACE.

Push the arc into position (see that the friction shoe does not stick out and prevent it going through), set up on the friction nut until it takes a strong pull to move the arc. Replace the stops, taking care that the one with the set screw is at the rear.

FEED BOX.

Weight of box for 10 cartridges, paper. .. 1-oz. 14-drs.
" " 20 " " .. 3½ " 1 "
" " 25 " " .. 4½ " ½ "
" " 20 " tin for drill 28 "
" " 25 " " " 34 "

This drawing shows five views of the Accles feed box.

Fig. 1.—Shows the box complete with cover on ready for storage. The cover is arranged with a loose flap, so that it can be readily torn off.

Fig. 2.—Shows the box with the cover torn off, and the position of the cartridges at the mouth of the box. At **A** & **B** are two narrow strips of strong paper arranged to prevent the cartridges from dropping out when the cover is removed. When the box is placed in the feeder, the feed wheels tear these away.

Fig. 3.—Shows the box with the tin guide strip partly drawn out, with the cartridges in their places.

Fig. 4.—Is a side view of the tin guide strip.

Fig. 5.—Is a view of the drill box, which is the same as the other boxes except that it is made of tin, and the guide strip is stronger. It is also arranged with a spring at **C** to hold the cartridges from dropping out when the box is turned mouth down.

The feed boxes are made of cardboard, equal in width and thickness to the length and diameter of the cartridge. On one side near the end it is partly cut away to let the feed wheels enter to grip the cartridge. On the other side are fixed two strips of cardboard to form a groove in which the corrugated tin strip slides.

When the first cartridge is caught by the feed wheels it is drawn out of the feed box, and with it the tin strip and all the cartridges in the box, each cartridge being presented in succession at regular distances and in perfect line to the feed mechanism. With this system, the movement of the cartridges is positive and regular, and they cannot possibly get out of line, or jam in feeding.

To remove the cover from the box, take the box in the left hand, with the mouth down, and the cover flap towards the right, take hold of the cover flap with the right hand and give a sudden downward movement, around the mouth and up the other side, so that the cover is torn clear off from the box.

AMMUNITION CASE.

Weight of case .. .. ..22 lbs.
Dimensions over all .. .. 16in. × 13in. × 12in.

This drawing shows the system of case or box used for storing and transporting the ammunition used with the Accles gun. The case is made of wood and lined with zinc. Round the top part of the zinc lining is arranged a narrow groove, which is filled with Beeswax or Luting. The zinc cover is flanged, so that when placed on the case it is pressed down into the wax or luting, and the case is then made air-tight by pressing more wax round it. The wood cover is then pressed down and locked, so no damp can get into the box, and the ammunition is easy to get at when required.

In packing the cases, the Accles feed boxes should be laid flat, so that the cartridges will lie on their sides, as in this position they will ride for any length of time without being damaged by the jolting of the carriage.

The case is made about $\frac{2}{8}$ inch longer than the cartridge box. To fill up this space a board is provided. When the case is full, and it is necessary to remove the feed boxes quickly from the case, the board is first drawn out, and so leaves space to get hold of the feed boxes quickly and easily.

The cases are provided with rope handles, held in place with cleats. There is no iron used in the make up of the cases, and they can be stored in the Magazine without danger.

These cases are arranged to fit into the Naval landing carriage, also into the Limber, and are also designed to take the ammunition direct from the Magazine to the gun. By this system, the cartridges do not have to be handled after being packed for storage until they are taken from the case and fed into the gun. The size of the case and weight when full depend on the calibre and size of the cartridges used.

GUN ON Y MOUNT.

Weight of gun	.. ..	150 lbs.
,, ,, Y mount	.. ..	26 lbs.
Extreme elevation	.. ..	50 deg.
,, depression	.. ..	50 deg.

This drawing shows the gun on the plain Y mount without shield. With this mount, the gun can be worked from any socket described in this book—Gun Carriage, Boat, Tripod, and all deck mountings.

GUN WITH SHIELD ON BULWARK SOCKET.

Weight of gun			..	..	150 lbs.
,,	,,	Y mount	..	..	31 ,,
,,	,,	shield	..	..	62 ,,
,,	,,	socket	..	..	26 ,,

This drawing shows the gun with shield mounted in socket on ship's bulwark or rail. These sockets should be placed at various parts of the ship so that the gun could be changed at any moment to that part of the ship where it would be of most service. The socket is made of gun metal, and held in place with bolts passing through the lower flange into or through the top rail of the bulwark.

GUN WITH SHIELD ON BULWARK BRACKET.

Weight of gun		..	..	150 lbs.
,,	,, Y mount	..	..	31 ,,
,,	,, shield	..	..	56 ,,
,,	,, bracket	..	..	36 ,,

This drawing shows the gun with shield mounted on ship's bulwarks with bracket. The bracket is made of gun metal, and is arranged to be secured against the upright plate of the bulwark with bolts. These brackets should be placed at various parts of the ship, so that the guns could be changed at any moment to that part of the ship where they would be of most service.

GUN WITH SHIELD ON DECK OR BRIDGE PEDESTAL.

Weight of gun			150 lbs.
,,	,, **Y** mount		31 ,,
,,	,, shield		56 ,,
,,	,, pedestal		131 ,,

This drawing shows the gun with shield mounted on deck or bridge pedestal. The pedestal is made of steel with a gun metal socket at the top to take the gun and mount. The lower part of the pedestal ends in an angle iron ring, through the flange of which pass the holding down bolts, by means of which it is fixed in position.

MAST HEAD MOUNT No. 1.

Weight of gun	150 lbs.
,, moving table and holding ring	104 ,,
,, mount	42 ,,
,, shield	92 ,,
Size of shield	36in. × 36in.
Thickness of shield	$\frac{1}{4}$in.
Degrees of elevation of gun	20°
,, depression	45°

This mount is designed for tops which have flat rails. It consists of a flat steel table mounted on four steel rollers, upon which it rolls along on top of the rail. The table, is provided with clips which grip under the outer edge of the rail. At the inner side of the rail, the table is provided with a binding handle, so that it may be clamped tight to the rail at any desired position. The shield is secured to the moving table, and moves round the mast head with it. In the centre of the table is fitted a holding ring with undercut grooves, into which the Y mount fits. The Y mount is so arranged that the gun can be given 15 degrees of right and left movement without moving the table.

The gun is arranged to have 40 degrees of depression, so it can at any time fire down on the deck, or at boats which may attempt to come alongside.

The easiest way to mount the gun in the top is to take it to pieces. Place the Y mount in the holding ring, then place the gun case in position, secure it to the arc, and bind it with the clamp handle. To make doubly sure that it will not move, bring the two arc stops close to the body of the Y mount and tighten, then put the gun together in the usual way.

NOTE.—Be sure that the friction nut (25E) on the Y mount is set up so that the gun will not move of itself, even when all the other clamps are loose. To secure the gun against damage from the movement of the ship, or the swaying of the mast head, remove the crank and pointing lever. Place the canvas cover on the gun (be sure that it is waterproof), depress the gun as far as it will go, bring the two arc stops close to the body of the Y mount and bind up tightly; also tighten the binding handle on Y mount and on the holding ring; should the clamps get loose the gun would take charge and get damaged. As the moving table has to carry the gun, shield and mount, and withstand the pressure of the wind, it is provided with locking screws to secure it firmly to the rail. These screws are set down with a spanner, and are only meant to secure the gun and mount against any chance of moving when not in use.

Plan and Elevation of No. 1 Mast head mounting, with Guns in position.

GUN MOUNTED ON BOAT MOUNT.

Weight of gun	..	..	150 lbs.
,, ,, Y mount	..	..	26 ,,
,, ,, pedestal	..	..	42 ,,
,, ,, holding ring and screws	..		$24\frac{1}{2}$,,

The boat mount consists of a holding ring and pedestal. The holding ring consists of a flat circular gun metal table with three raised under-cut sections, a binding handle and block. This ring is designed so that one can be placed at each end of the boat. It is embedded in the seat of the boat, so that the raised sections are flush with the top, thus leaving the seat flat and even.

The pedestal is made of gun metal with a flat bottom, cut away in three places to fit into and lock under the raised sections of the holding ring. When placed in the holding ring, it is given a one-third turn, and the locking block put into position and clamped up with the binding handle. The top of the pedestal ends in a socket into which the stem of the Y mount fits. All boats intended to take machine guns should be fitted with a holding ring at each end, so that the gun could be placed at either end of the boat, as the case required. When making a landing, the gun should be placed in the bow of the boat; upon embarking, it should be in the stern. When using the boat without the gun, the pedestal should be removed from the holding ring and stored in a convenient place in the boat, where it would be out of the way. The pedestal should never be taken away from the boat.

GUN MOUNTED IN BOAT.

This drawing shews an elevation and plan of a boat with a gun mounted in the bow, and a holding ring at the stern.

PEDESTAL MOUNT. Fig. 1.

Weight .. .. .. 131 lbs.
Height .. .. .. 36 inches.

The pedestal mount consists of a cone made of $\frac{1}{4}$ inch steel plates, strengthened at the base by an angle iron ring, through the flange of which the holding down bolts pass. The top of the pedestal ends in a gun metal socket (with clamping handle) into which the stem of the Y mount enters, carrying the gun and shield.

This pedestal is designed for use on ship's bridges, and various other parts of ships and boats where there are no bulwarks or other means of mounting the gun.

BOAT PEDESTAL, Fig. 2.

Weight .. .. 42 lbs.

This pedestal is made of gun metal, with a flat bottom, cut away in three places to fit into, and lock under the raised section of the holding ring. When placed in the holding ring, it is given a one-third turn and the locking block put into position and clamped up with a binding handle. The top of the Pedestal ends in a socket, into which the stem of the Y mount fits, and is clamped up with a binding handle.

HOLDING RING, Fig. 3.

Weight ... . $24\frac{1}{2}$ lbs.

The holding ring consists of a flat circular gun metal table with three raised undercut sections, a binding handle and locking block. The ring is designed so that one can be placed at each end of the boat. It is embedded in the seat of the boat, so that the raised sections are flush with the top, thus leaving the seat flat and even.

BULWARK BRACKET. Fig. 4.

Weight .. .. .. 33 lbs.

The bulwark bracket is made of gun metal. and is arranged with a socket hole and binding clamp to take the Y mount. This bracket is designed to be secured against the side of the Bulwark.

BULWARK SOCKET Fig. 5.

Weight .. .. .. 26 lbs.

The bulwark socket is made of gun metal. The socket is provided with a flange at the bottom, through which the holding down bolts pass to secure it on any desired place.

NAVAL LANDING CARRIAGE.

Width of track	3ft. 10in.
Height of wheel	3ft. 9in.
Length of trail	5ft. 4in.
Length over all	6ft. 9in.
Width over all	5ft.
Size of Ammunition box	14in x 13in. x 11in.
Weight of carriage frame	183 lbs.
,, two wheels	126 lbs.
,, Ammunition box empty	22 lbs.
,, ,, ,, full	100 lbs.
,, tools and accessories	28 lbs.

The carriage consists of a frame and trail made of steel, mounted on a hollow steel axle.

The trail is provided with a folding seat and a movable tool box. Attached to the under part of the trail is a shovel, and at the front end is a combination pick and axe.

On each side of the gun is space for two wooden ammunition cases; each case will hold 1000 rounds, making in all 4000 cartridges with the gun. Between the trail cheeks, just to the rear of the axle, is fitted a gun-metal socket, into which the Y mount of the gun enters. On top of this socket two plates are arranged so that they can be set to limit the horizontal oscillation to any required degree.

A movable cross bar is arranged to fit into eyes at the end of the trail for two men to hold and guide the carriage when on the move. Two drag ropes and six pulling belts are provided. The ropes are fitted with a piece of chain at one end to prevent them being cut by the wheels. The chain end of the rope hooks into eye washers at the end of the axle. The carriage is well balanced and easy running.

For storage on board ship, the ammunition cases are removed to the magazine, and the wheels are taken off, and laid and tied on to the frame, making a package 6ft. 6in. x 5ft. x 16in., which will weigh 309 lbs.

The ammunition case is made of wood with brass hinges and clasps, rope handles, and lined with zinc. The top part of the zinc lining is provided with a groove all round, into which a flanged zinc cover fits, so that it can be made airtight by filling the groove with wax. These cases are designed for storing the ammunition in the ship's magazine, and are so arranged that they can be taken direct from the magazine and placed on the gun carriage, or to any part of the ship where the gun is being used. They are replaced in the magazine when the firing is done.

TWO-WHEELED NAVAL LANDING CARRIAGE.

This drawing shows the carriage taken to pieces and packed for storage when on board ship. The carriage takes up a space of 6ft. 6in. × 5ft. × 16in., and weighs 309 lbs. including the entrenching tools.

TO DISMOUNT THE CARRIAGE.

Take off the Ammunition boxes, and place in the magazine. Remove the gun, remove the tool box, and place in the gunner's store. Place the trail cross-bar in position alongside the trail and secure with strap, fold up the drag ropes and pulling belts, and secure between cheek of the trail at rear of axle. Remove the linch pins and hook washers. One man stands at each wheel, one man at front of carriage frame. When all is ready the man at the front of the carriage lifts it, and the two men at the wheels draw them off. The frame is then laid on the deck, the hook washers and linch pins replaced in the axle and secured, so that there will be no danger of their being knocked out and lost. Place one wheel dish side down on the trail, so that the rim of the wheel comes against the trail eye at the rear end in such a position that the outer end of the spoke comes over the trail cheek. Place the second wheel dish side down over the first wheel, so that the hub of the first wheel and the mount socket will pass between the spokes of the second wheel and allow it to lie flat, and then secure with pieces of rope at the points **B. C.** and **A.** The bright part of the axle should be well covered with tallow before storage.

In putting the carriage together, the same directions are followed as for taking to pieces, but in inverse order.

LIMBER FOR NAVAL LANDING CARRIAGE.

Width of track	3 ft. 10 in.
Total length including pole	10 ,, 3 ,,
,, width over all	4 ,, 9 ,,
Length of same with pole removed	4 ,, 0 ,,
Diameter of wheels	4 ,, 0 ,,
Weight of frame	184 lbs.
,, wheels	126 ,,
,, pole	26 ,,
,, tools and accessories	16 ,,
Number of rounds of ammunition carried	6000 to 8000
,, ,, ,, cases	6 or 8
Total weight of cases empty	96 lbs.
,, ,, full	576 ,,
Number of men required	12

The limber consists of a steel frame mounted on a hollow steel axle by two elliptical springs, and arranged with a long pole running from the centre of the frame, and is provided with two cross bars by means of which four men can push and guide it along. The frame is arranged to carry six or eight ammunition cases holding 1000 rounds of cartridge each, making in all 6000 or 8000 rounds carried on the limber. The limber is provided with two shovels, two drag ropes and six pulling belts. The frame is arranged at the rear with a hook on which the trail of the gun carriage can be hooked. The limber is also fitted with folding racks for carrying the rifles, while the men are dragging the limber. The limber is arranged so that it can be drawn by horses or mules when convenient.

The limber is arranged so that it can be easily taken to pieces and stored when on board ship.

This limber can be used for many other purposes beside transporting ammunition. It can be used for carrying luggage, ropes, tools, and many other things that require transporting on shore in connection with landing parties.

THREE-WHEELED UNIVERSAL CARRIAGE.

Weight of Gun	...	...	...	146 lbs.
,, ,, Mount	...	...	...	32 ,,
,, ,, Carriage and Wheels	...	...	480 ,,
,, ,, Ammunition Boxes, empty		...	96 ,,
,, ,, ,, ,, full	...	...	558 ,,
,, ,, Tools and equipment	...	...	48 ,,

Number of Cartridges carried on the carriage, 6,000

This Carriage has three wheels, two main wheels in front, and a smaller guide wheel at the rear.

The body of the carriage is supported by the two large wheels.

The rear end of the trail is bent up forming an arch, under which the guide wheel is pivoted so that it can turn freely under the arch while the carriage is in motion. The frame and trail of the carriage are light and strong, and are made of angle steel.

The gun is mounted on a small steel pedestal placed just to the rear of the axle, on the trail, and is high enough to allow the gun to have an all-round fire above the wheels.

The ammunition is carried in cases placed on each side of the gun, on the platform of the carriage.

A set of entrenching tools is provided, and is carried underneath the platform of the carriage.

The other tools and spare parts belonging to the gun are carried in a small box let in between the cheeks of the trial.

Two drag ropes and six pulling belts are provided with the carriage, also two pushing poles. When required, a tripod can be carried on the front of the carriage, to be used as a mount for the Gun in positions inaccessible to the carriage. With this carriage the gun is always ready for instant use and can be fired while in motion, whether advancing or retreating. As two poles are provided, fitting into sockets on each side of the carriage, with which it can be pushed to the front, the men need never get before the Gun during advancing fire.

This construction of carriage and mount, giving an all-round fire, the gun can be brought to bear instantly upon any point, without moving the carriage.

The ability to fire the Gun while retreating or advancing is a very essential feature in machine guns, particularly when they are called upon to maintain a continuous fire in close contests. Oftentimes a change of base becomes necessary ; but to stop the firing might prove disastrous.

With the Gun mounted on this carriage, an effective fire can be maintained while the carriage is being moved, so that no time is lost and no weak places are left exposed by the gun being thrown out of action.

Another feature of this carriage is that the attachments of the small wheel are so constructed that the wheel can be unshipped with great rapidity. This allows the trail to come to the ground, and permits of a much greater elevation of fire.

From the axle of the small wheel a rod is taken terminating in a cross bar. This serves to operate the guide wheel, and, together with a drag rope hooked to the end of the trail to pull the carriage along.

The Gun detachment should consist of an officer and ten men; each man should have a rifle provided with a sling. The men would be divided up as follows : —on the march, three men at each drag rope, two men at the drawing bar, and two men as relief and to assist at the wheels over rough ground.

At the firing position the arrangement would be as follows :—one man at the crank, one man to feed, one man to point and fire, and one man to stand by to relieve any of the others in case of accident. The other six would be using their rifles when not required in connection with the moving of the carriage.

Ten men can take the gun over ordinary country roads and lanes. In rough and broken country devoid of roads, 6 extra men would be required, with additional drag ropes, to transport the Gun with reasonable ease and despatch. These six men when not employed in moving the Gun and carriage would be engaged in using their rifles.

The ammunition used by this detachment could be taken from the Gun ammunition on the carriage, as their rifles would be of the same calibre as the Gun, or arrangements could be made to carry the ammunition allotted to each man, on the carriage.

FIELD CARRIAGE AND LIMBER

FOR THE

ACCLES MACHINE GUN.

Weight of Gun			150 lbs.
,,	Carriage		420 ,,
,,	Mount		25 ,,
,,	Shield		240 ,,
,	2 Ammunition Cases, empty		52 ,,
,,	,, ,, full		154 ,,
,,	Limber		370 ,,
,,	Ammunition Case, empty		96 ,,
,,	,, ,, full		712 ,,
,,	Equipment		40 ,,

Amount of Ammunition carried with Gun, (·303″) 10000 rounds.

The carriage is constructed of steel, and is made strong enough to stand the rough usage of Field Service. The Gun is mounted on the trail, in the centre of the carriage, close up behind the axle. The carriage is provided with a folding shield of steel, which covers the whole width of the carriage between the wheels, and is five feet, ten inches in height. This shield effectually protects the Gunners from Rifle shots whilst in action. When on the march, the top of the shield folds down and forms a seat for the Gunners, and the lower part turns up, forming a foot rest. The carriage is arranged to carry two ammunition cases holding 2000 rounds of ammunition, one case being placed on each side of the Gun. The trail is provided with a seat for the Gunner, and a tool box is also fitted in the trail. The whole is mounted on a solid steel axle, and is carried upon two substantial wheels of the regulation service pattern.

The frame of the Limber is constructed of angle steel, on top of which is mounted a steel ammunition case, arranged to hold 8000 rounds of ammunition. The top of the ammunition case forms a seat for three Gunners. The Limber can be arranged with either pole or shafts.

The Gun detachment should consist of five men divided as follows:—one man to point the Gun, one man to turn the crank, one man to feed the cartridges into the Gun, the other two men would keep him supplied with cartridges from the Limber, and at any time change places with any of the men working the Gun when a relief was necessary. All the five men should be so instructed that they could perform any of the duties connected with the working of the Gun. When on the march two men would sit on the Gun carriage, one on each side of the Gun and three on the Limber. If required, a third man could ride on the Gun Carriage.

TRIPOD MOUNTING.

Weight .. .. .. 44 lbs.

The legs of the tripod are made of steel tube, with round dished or cupped feet at the bottom; they are arranged in this way so as to stand firm on soft ground, and are also arranged with a cone spike or point in the centre of the feet to prevent slipping on hard ground or boards.

The upper end of the legs are hinged into a gun metal socket, into which the stem of the Y mount enters. The upper part of the legs where they are hinged to the socket, are arranged with wings on the inner side, which pass into the socket through slots when the legs are closed together. When the legs are spread, these wings are drawn out of the socket so that the stem of the Y mount can enter. When the stem of the Y mount is in the socket, the wings cannot enter the socket and so prevent the legs from closing up while the gun is mounted. For use on ship board, broad wooden shoes are fitted to the feet and are provided with india-rubber rings at the bottom, which prevent the gun and tripod from slipping, and also from marking the deck.

One leg of the tripod unscrews, and is arranged to carry all the tools and spare parts.

GUN MOUNTED ON CHINESE WHEELBARROW

Weight of barrow .. .. .. 146 lbs.
Two Ammunition boxes .. .. .. 64 ,,

In many parts of China, wheelbarrows of the type shewn in this drawing are used for transporting goods from place to place. This system of transport is the most suitable in the parts of China where used, as the roads and streets are so narrow that ordinary vehicles could not pass over or through them. Therefore, to make the gun servicable where such conditions exist, it has been mounted on the Chinese transport wheelbarrow. When travelling, the gun is removed from the top of the barrow and placed across it just behind the wheel.

Two boxes of 2000 rounds each of ammunition are carried on the barrow, one on each side of the wheel. On the front end of the barrow is carried a tripod. On the top rail of the barrow is fitted a gun metal socket into which the gun mount fits with the gun during firing. With one of these barrows one man will transport at a quick walk for eight hours a day from 600 to 800 pounds over ordinary roads.

TURRET MOUNTING.

Weight of gun	.. .. ..	220 lbs.
,, mount	.. .. ..	118 ,,

This drawing shows the system of mounting arranged for disappearing turrets. The mount consists of two flat steel tables. The under one is hinged to the side of the turret in front of the port-hole, and is held up at the rear by the elevating screw. The gun is mounted on the upper table, and held in place by the trunnion arms. The upper table slides on the under one. When the turret is raised to the firing position, the gun is pushed forward by sliding the upper table along the under one until the muzzle of the gun has passed out through the port-hole of the turret, at which time a stop bolt springs up and prevents the gun from moving back while firing. To prevent the turret from being lowered while the gun is run out, a bolt is arranged just under the port-hole, this is pushed out through the side of the turret through a small hole, by the forward movement of the gun, and is held there until the gun is run in, at which time the bolt is returned by a spring. The upper table is so arranged that at the firing point it has a right and left movement of 30 degrees. The gun can be given 15 degrees of depression and 30 degrees of elevation.

In order not to raise the turret above the ground more than is necessary, the gun is mounted close up to the top.

The gun is arranged with the feeder on the top, and the cartridges are fed in horizontally from the right hand side. The crank is placed on the left side, and the pointing lever on the right.

Three men are required to work the gun. No. 1 directs and points the gun. No. 2 attends to the supplying of ammunition to the gun. No. 3 turns the crank.

It is the duty of No. 1 to see that the gun is kept in proper working order. It is No. 2's duty to see that there is a proper supply of ammunition in the turret, and that it is in a position to be quickly fed to the gun. No. 3 sees that the crank is in position ready for action. (No. 3 should assist No. 2 in bringing the ammunition into the turret from the magazine)

When all is in proper order, the turret is raised to the firing position.

No. 1 takes his place at the rear of the gun.
No. 2 at the right hand side.
No. 3 at the left hand side.

Nos. 2 and 3 run the gun out. No. 1 brings the gun into line by working the elevating screw with his right hand and turning the turret by means of the wheel A with his left hand. When in approximate line, No. 1 lets go the wheel A. and directs the gun by means of the pointing lever, which passes under his right arm. At the same time he grasps the trigger handle with his right hand.

No. 2 places a box of cartridges into the feeder. No. 3 turns the crank. When No. 1 gets the gun on the mark he presses the trigger and fires the gun. No. 2 replaces the feed boxes as fast as they are emptied by the gun.

When the firing is stopped (if it is not to be resumed at once) the gun should be cleared of all the cartridges which have not been fired. To do so No. 2 lifts the feeder out of the gun (and with it most of the cartridges) and removes them from the feeder, pulling out the tin strip which will draw out all the cartridges with it. No. 1 presses down the trigger and turns the safety cam to " safe."

No. 3 turns the crank backward, watches the receiver, and picks out the cartridges and empty shells as they are drawn out by the locks, until the gun is clear.

No 2 presses down the stop bolt and holds it while Nos. 1 and 3 run the gun in. The turret is then lowered into position.

No. 1 removes the locks from the gun. No. 2 rearranges the ammunition and the empty boxes and tin strips.

No. 3 proceeds to clean the gun.

The gun can be cleaned through the breech by passing the cleaning rod through the lockport and receiver into the barrel after the locks have been removed. To clean the gun from the front end, it would be necessary to raise the turret and run out the gun and clean it from the outside of the turret.

This is the most advisable way.

The gun should always be cleared of any cartridges that may be left in it when the firing is stopped, before the turret is lowered.

If possible, No. 1 should stop No. 2 from feeding the gun just before stopping the firing so as to have no cartridges left in the gun when finished.

It would be the safest plan to fire all the cartridges that may be in the gun after the order to cease firing is given. Or the safety cam could be turned to "safe" and all the cartridges run through the gun. In this case, two cartridges only would be fired.

No. 1 should be held responsible for the proper working of the gun. He should never leave the gun after firing until he has seen all the cartridges removed from it, and has satisfied himself by examination that there are no cartridges left in the gun or feeder. He should then assure himself that the safety cam is at safe, and before leaving see that no live cartridges are left in the turret.

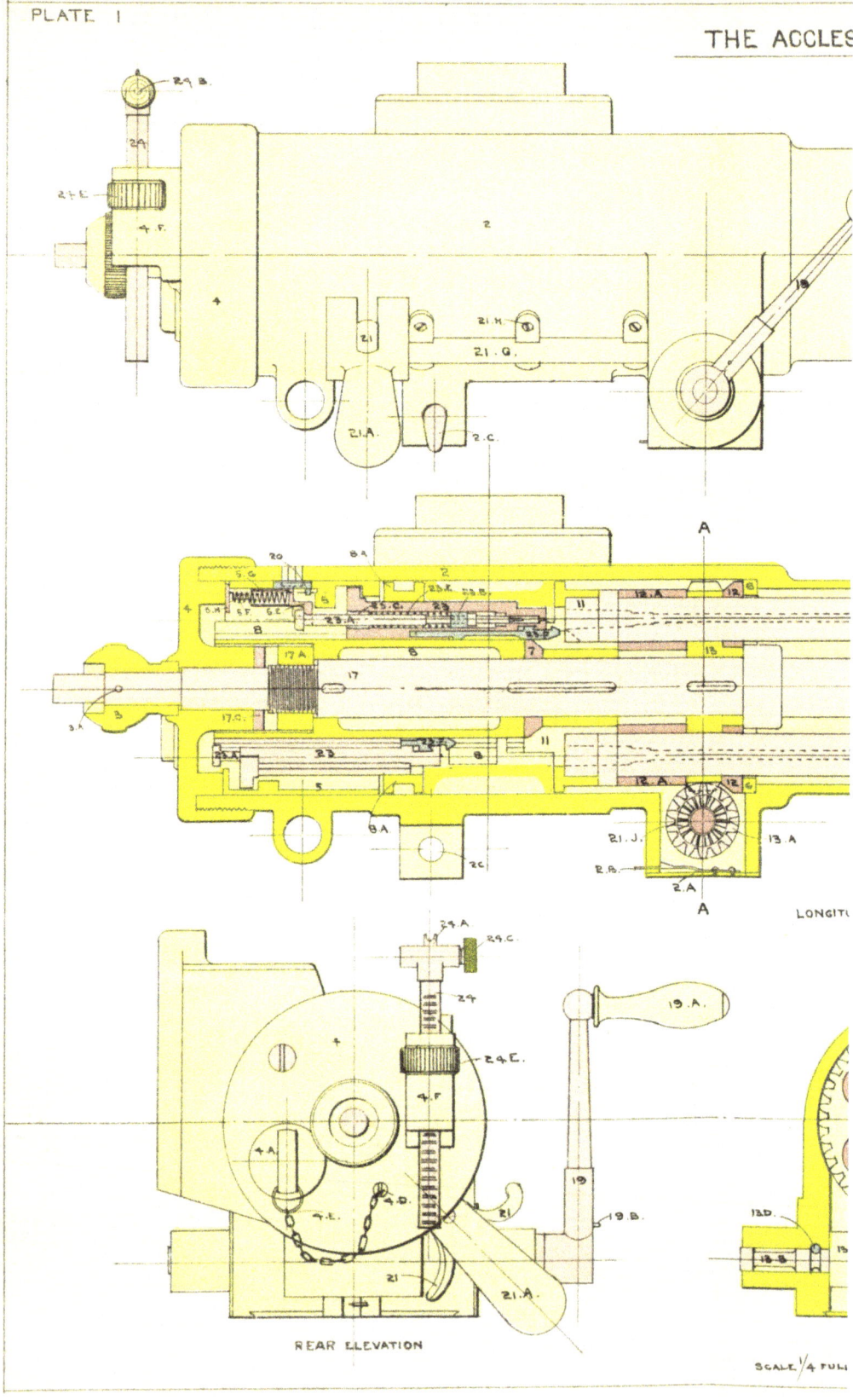

PLATE 1

THE ACCLES

LONGITU

REAR ELEVATION

SCALE 1/4 FULL

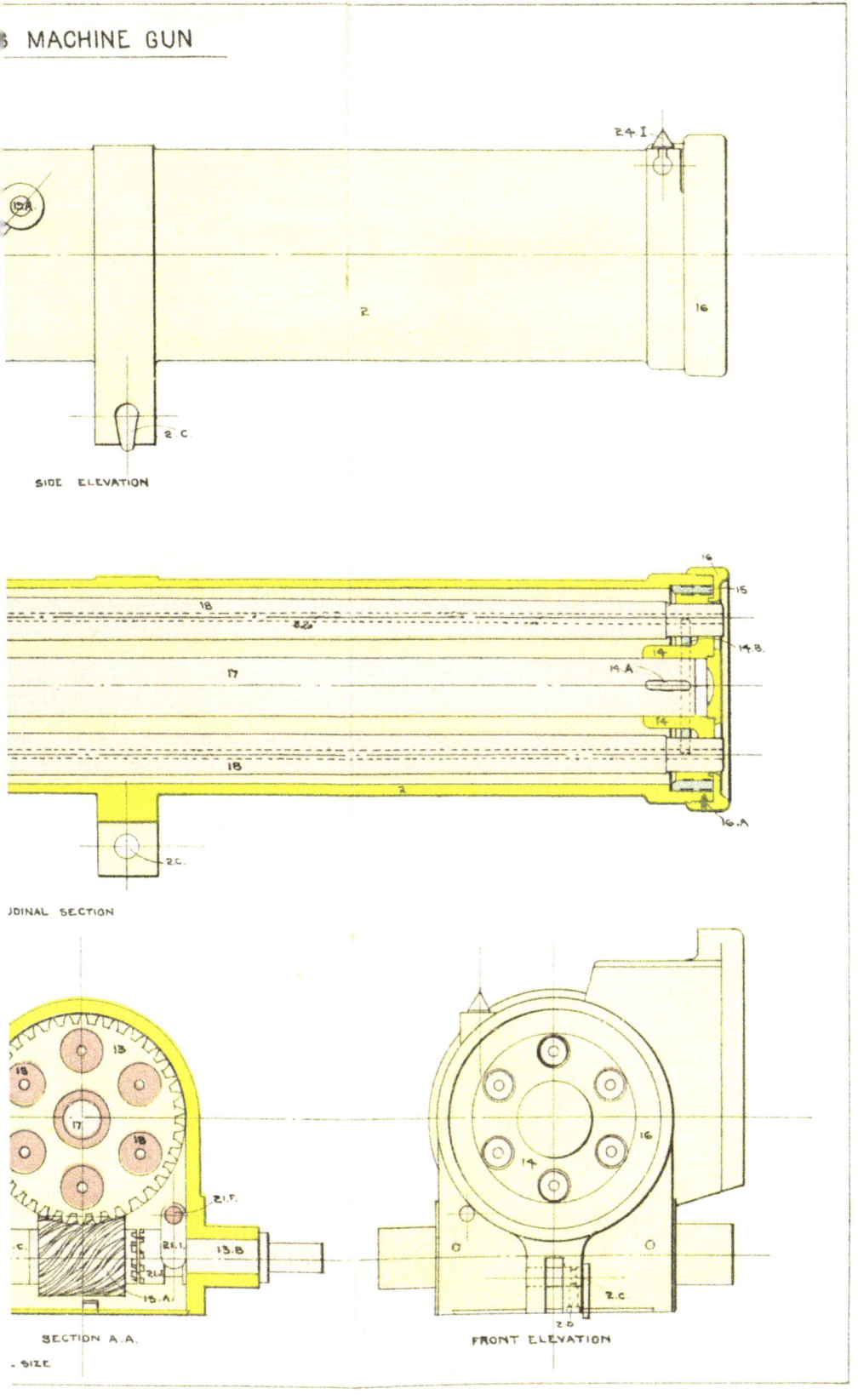

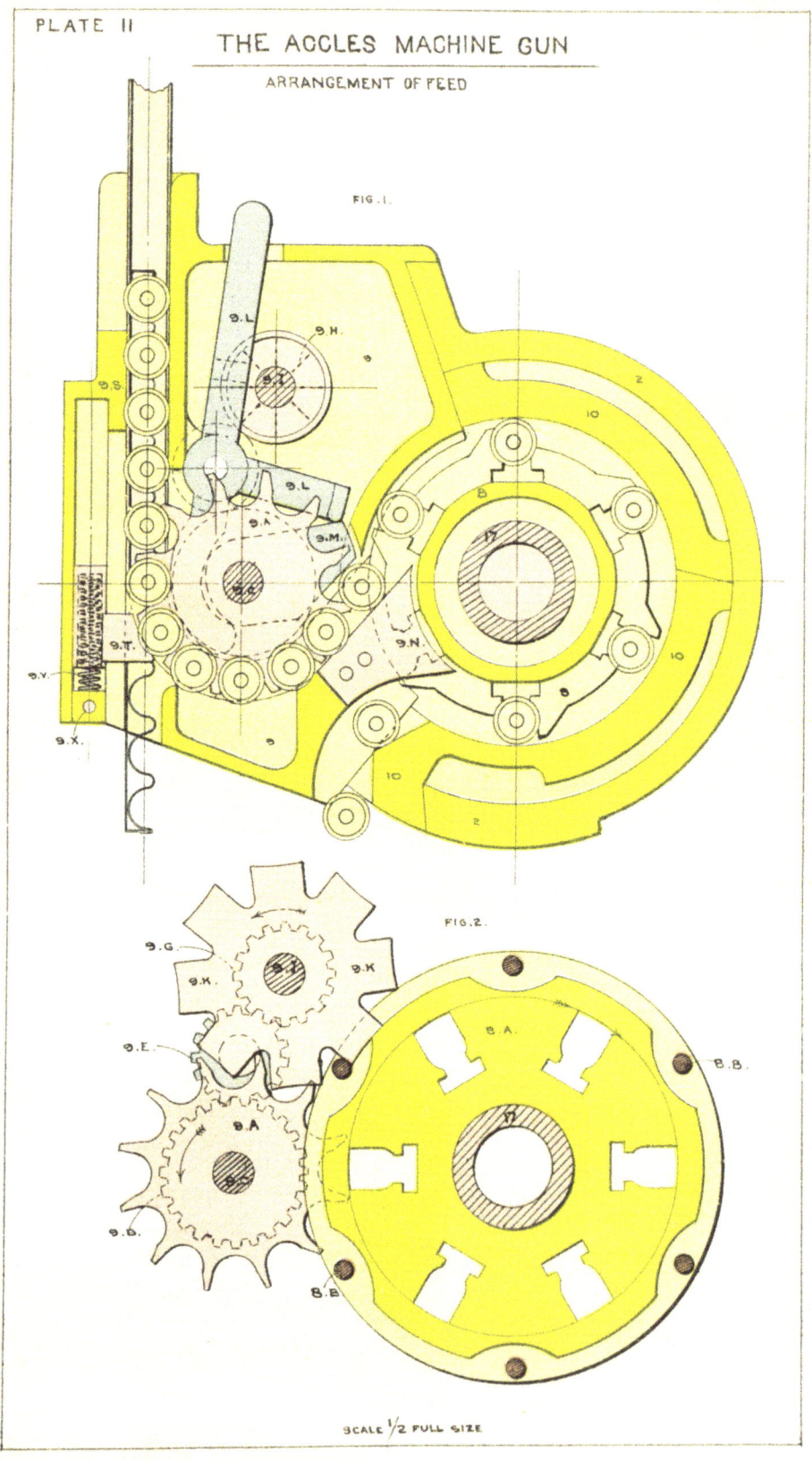

PLATE III

THE ACCLES MACHINE GUN

GUN ON Y MOUNT

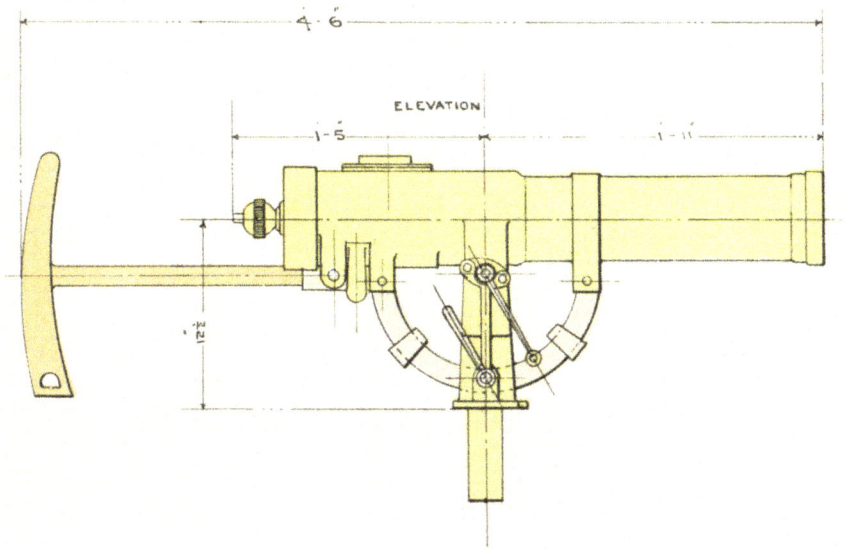

ELEVATION

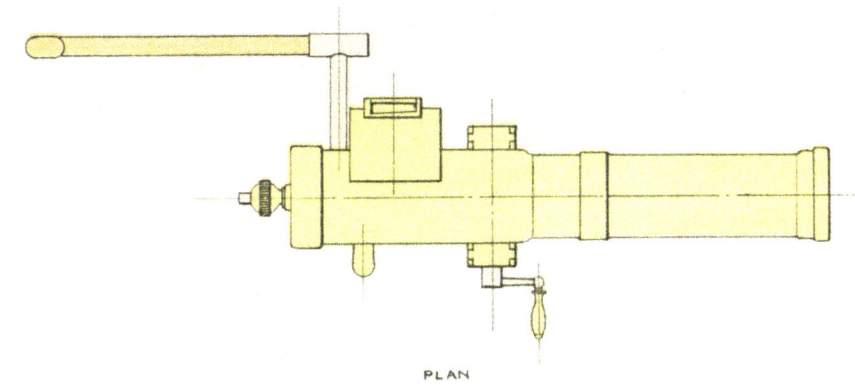

PLAN

SCALE 1/12 FULL SIZE

PLATE IV

THE ACCLES MACHINE GUN

GUN WITH SHIELD ON BULWARK SOCKET

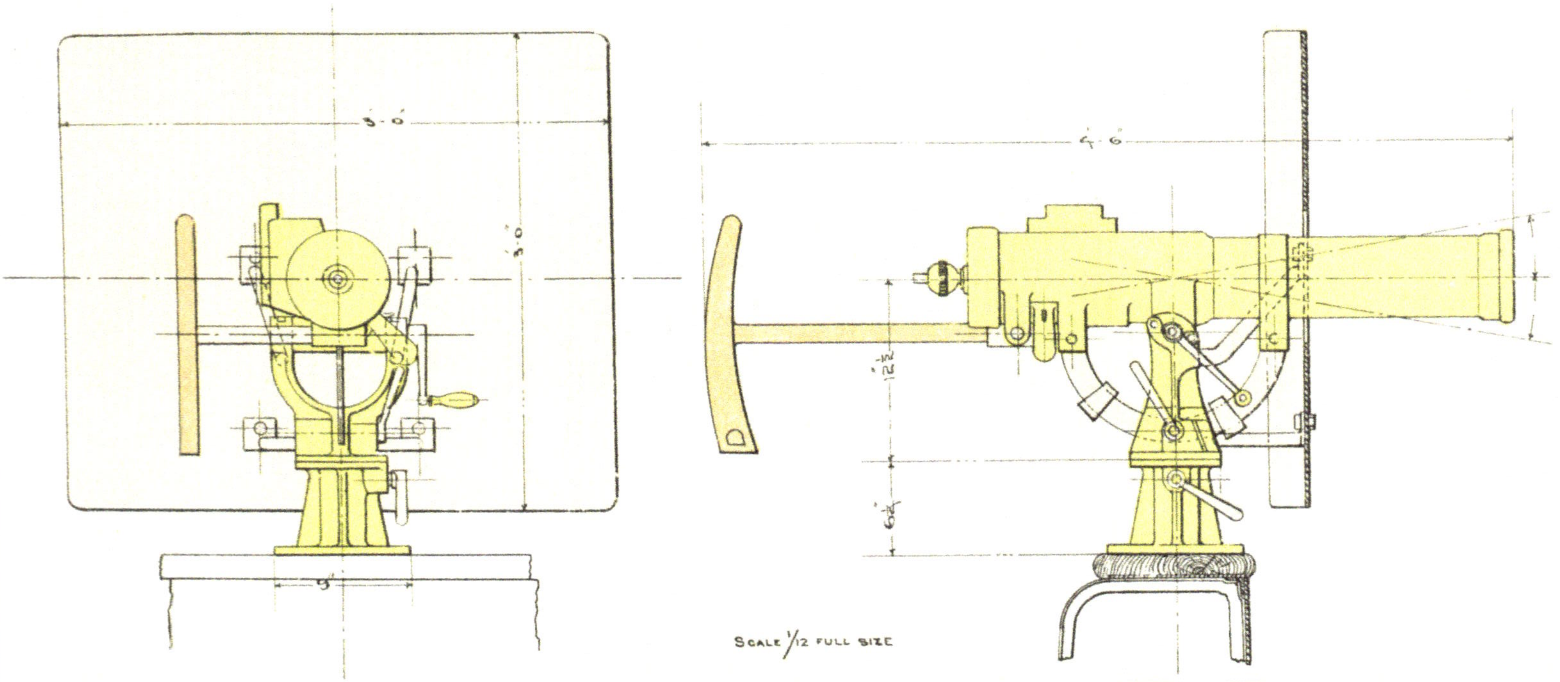

Scale 1/2 Full Size

PLATE V

THE ACCLES MACHINE GUN

GUN WITH SHIELD ON BULWARK BRACKET

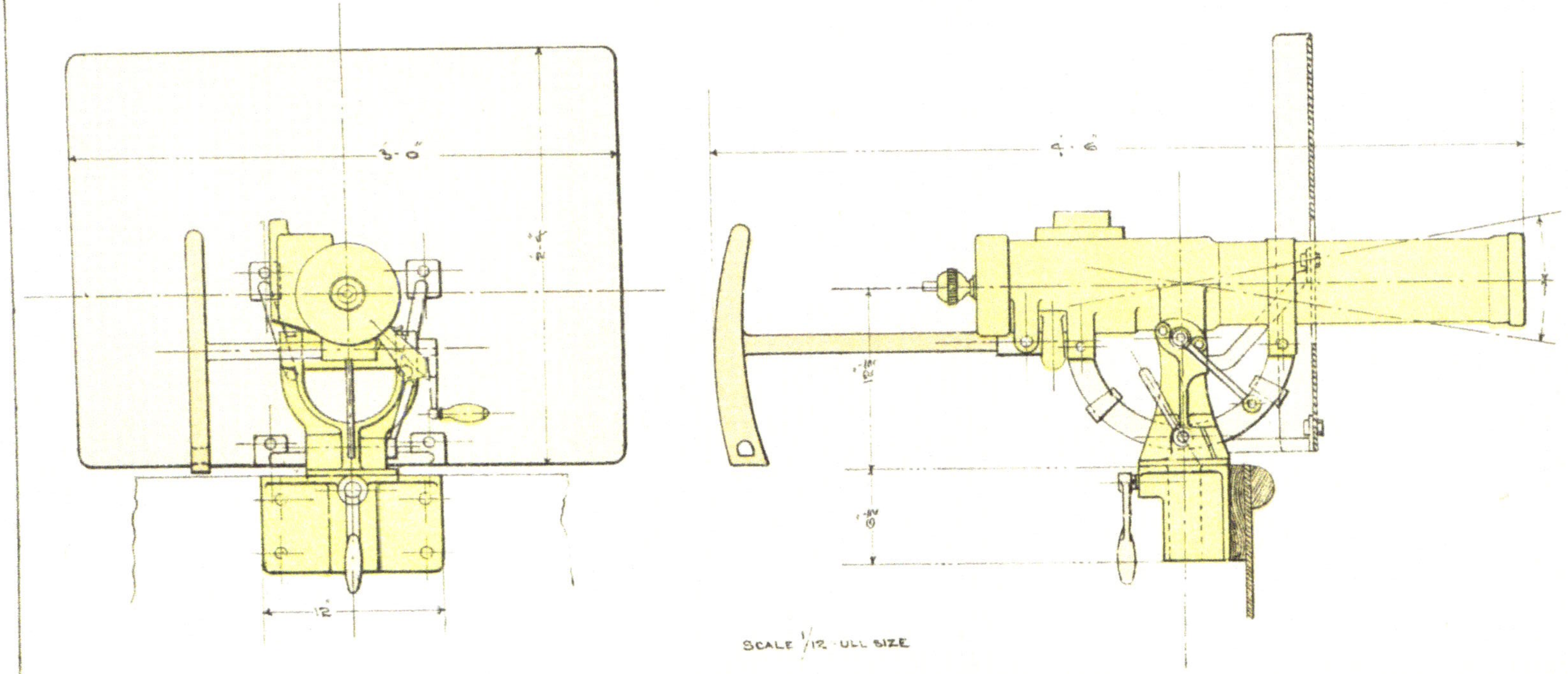

SCALE 1/12 FULL SIZE

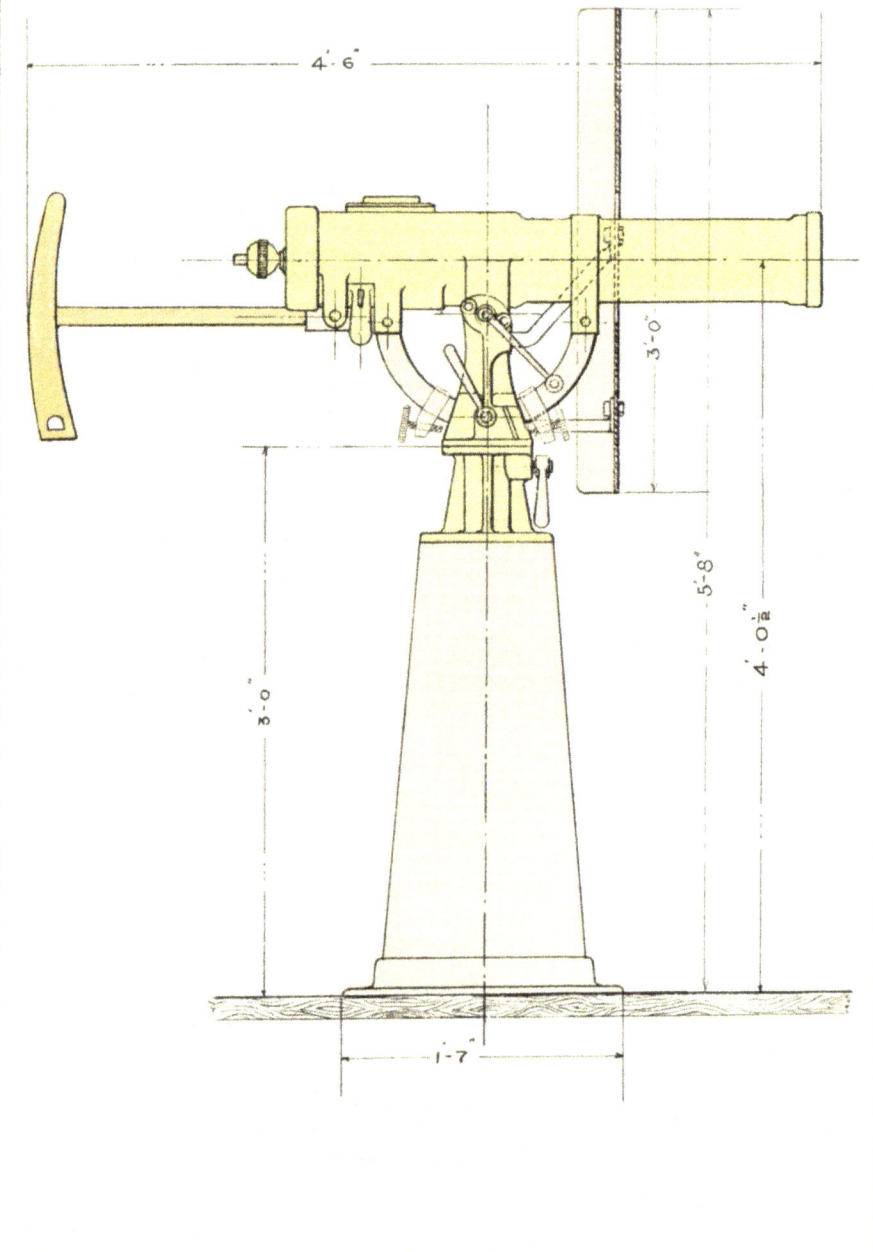

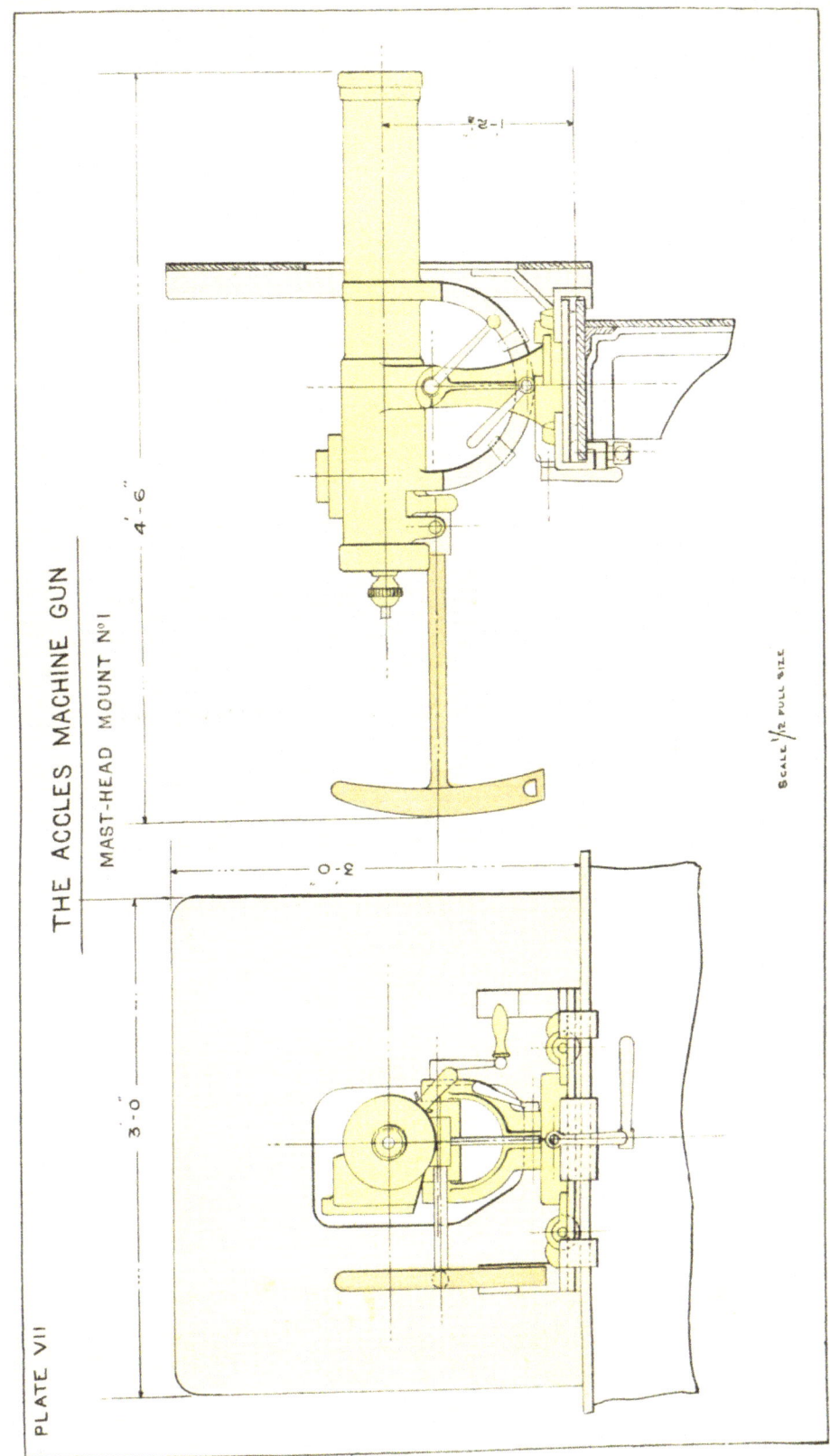

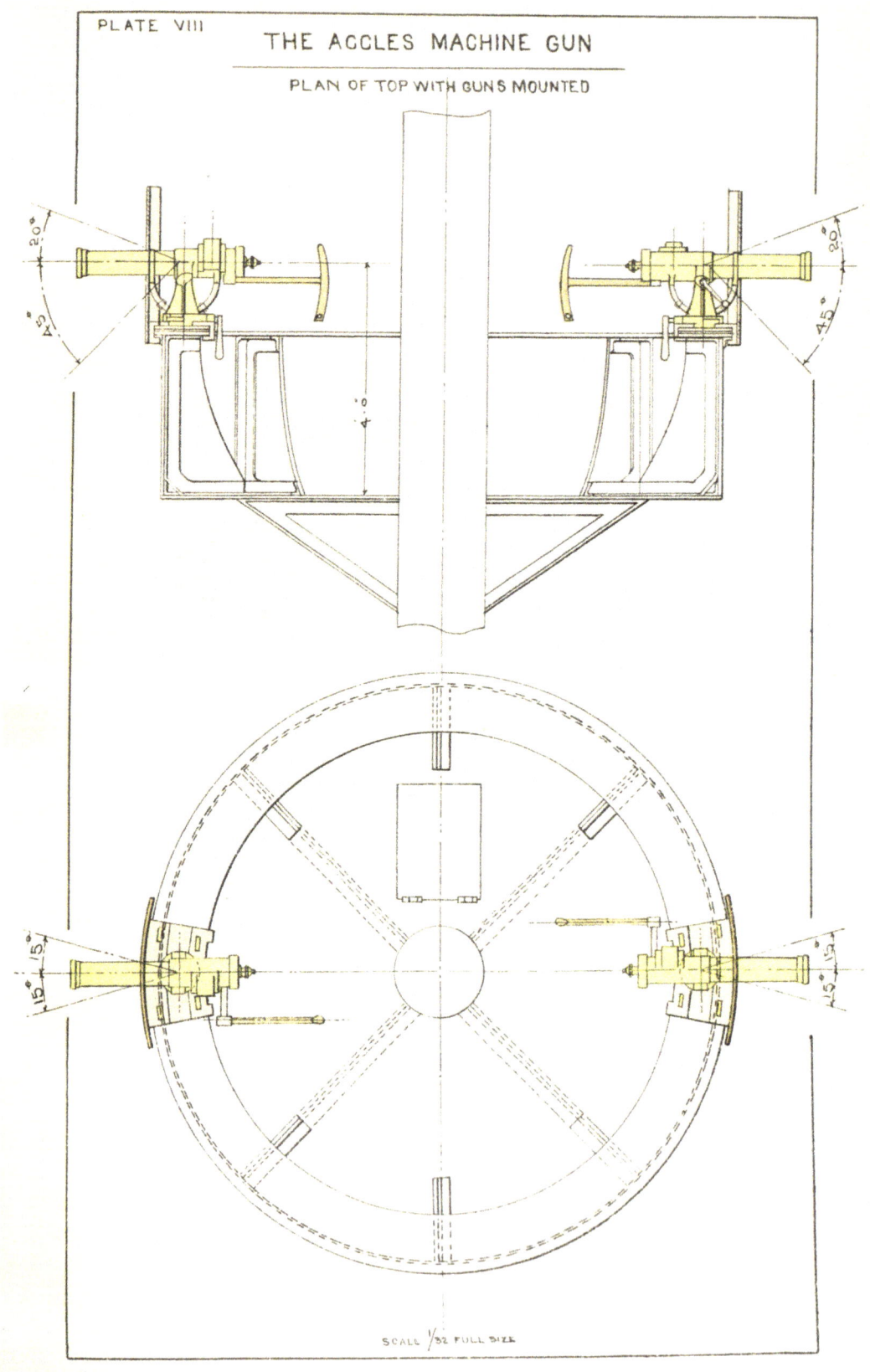

PLATE XI

THE ACCLES MACHINE GUN

GUN MOUNTED ON BOAT MOUNT

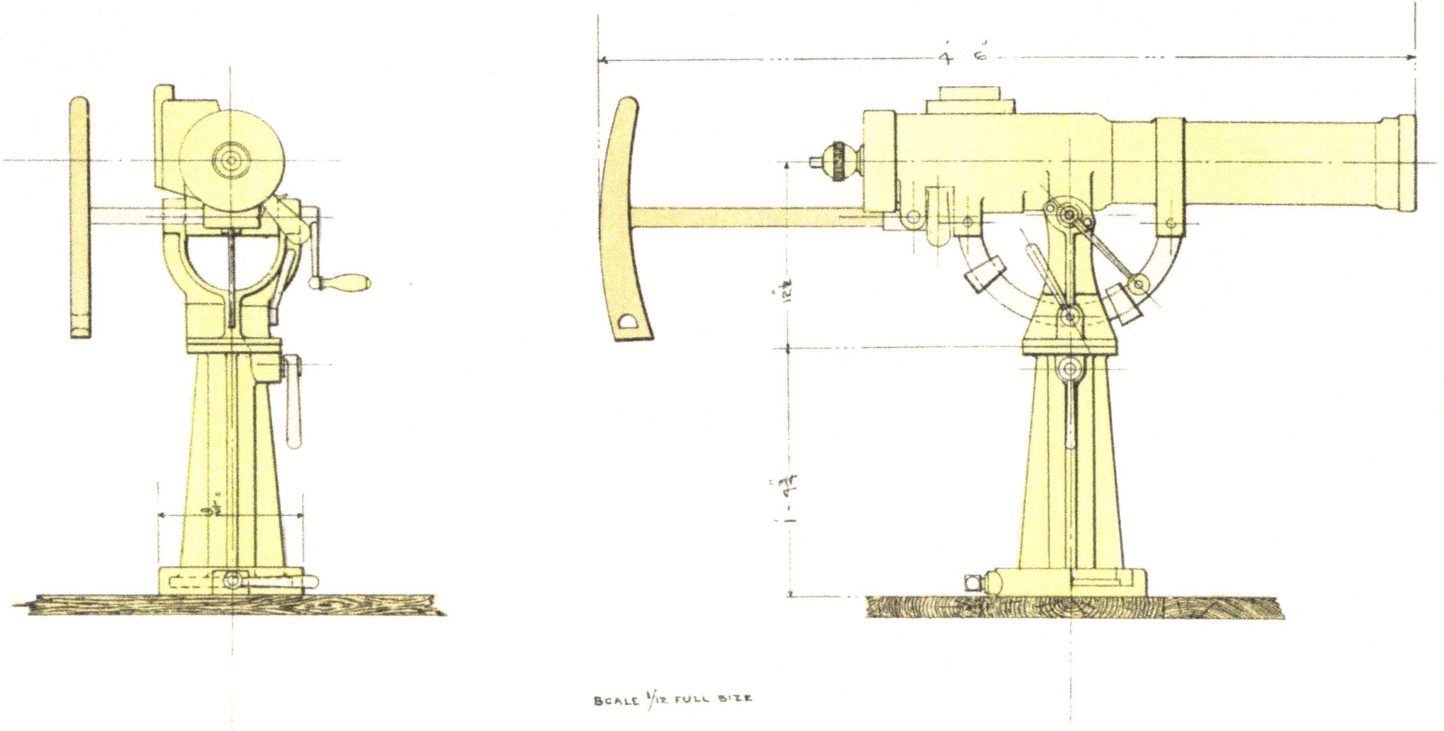

SCALE 1/12 FULL SIZE

PLATE XII

THE ACCLES MACHINE GUN

BOAT WITH GUN MOUNTED

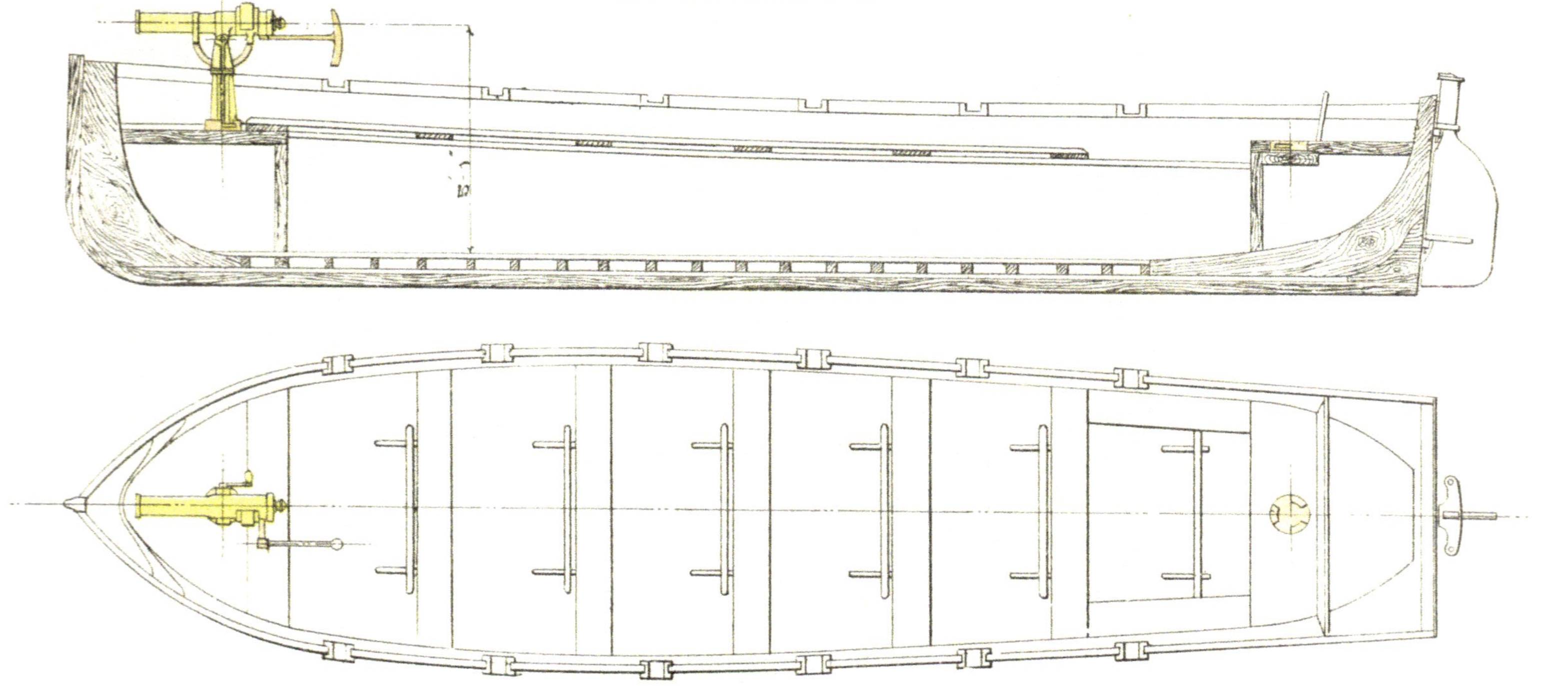

SCALE 1/48 FULL SIZE

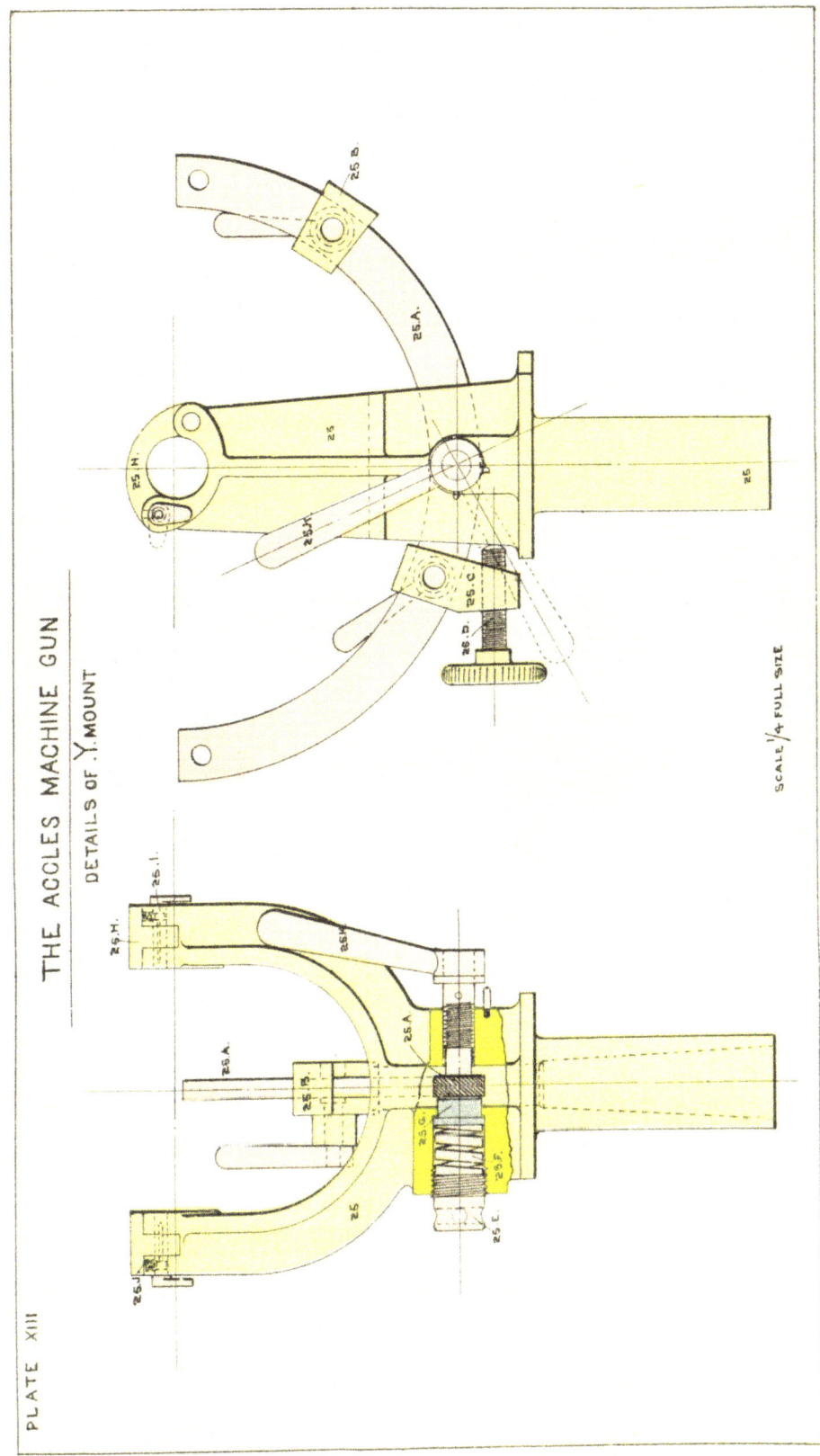

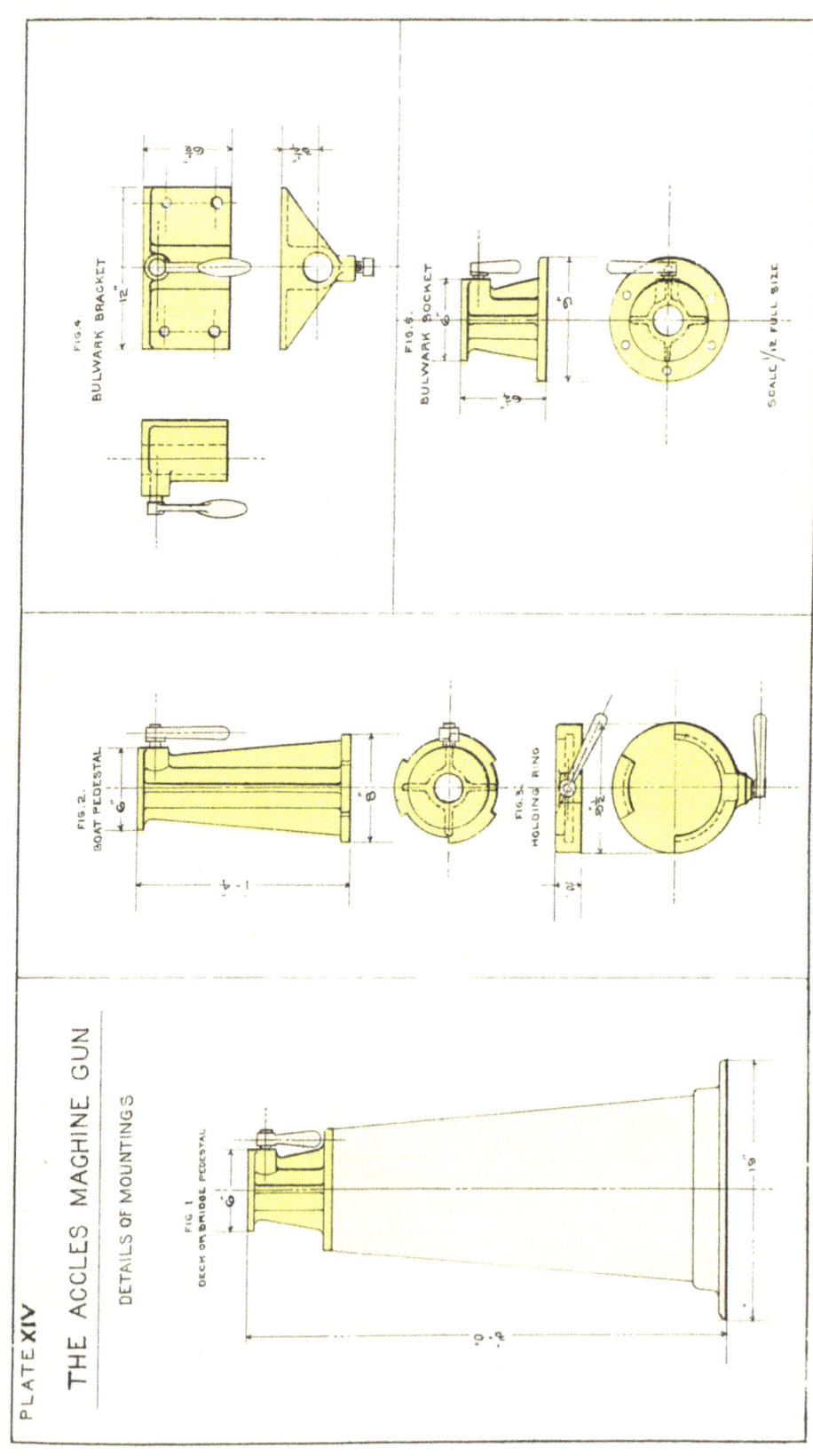

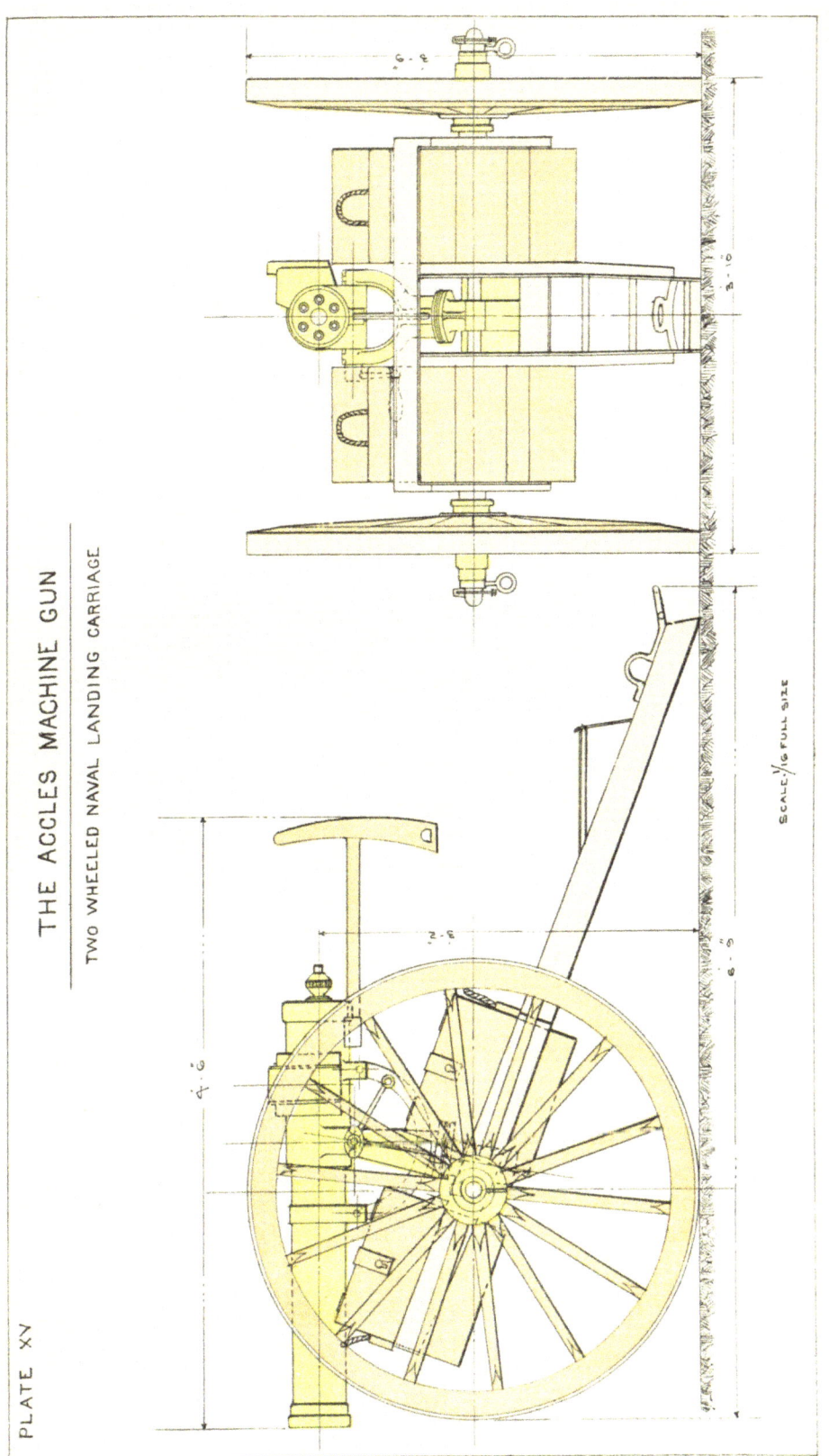

PLATE XVI

THE ACCLES MACHINE GUN
TWO WHEELED NAVAL LANDING CARRIAGE IN STOWING POSITION

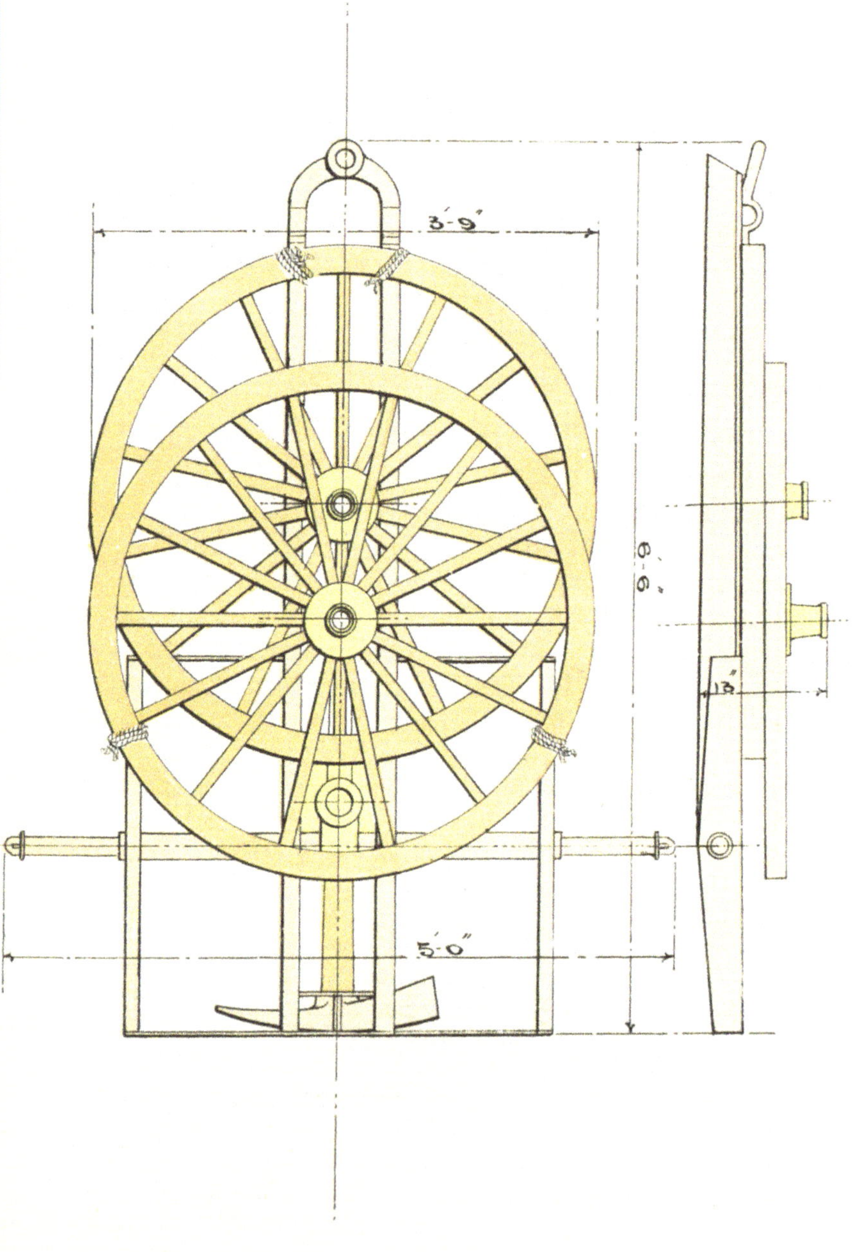

SCALE 1/16 FULL SIZE

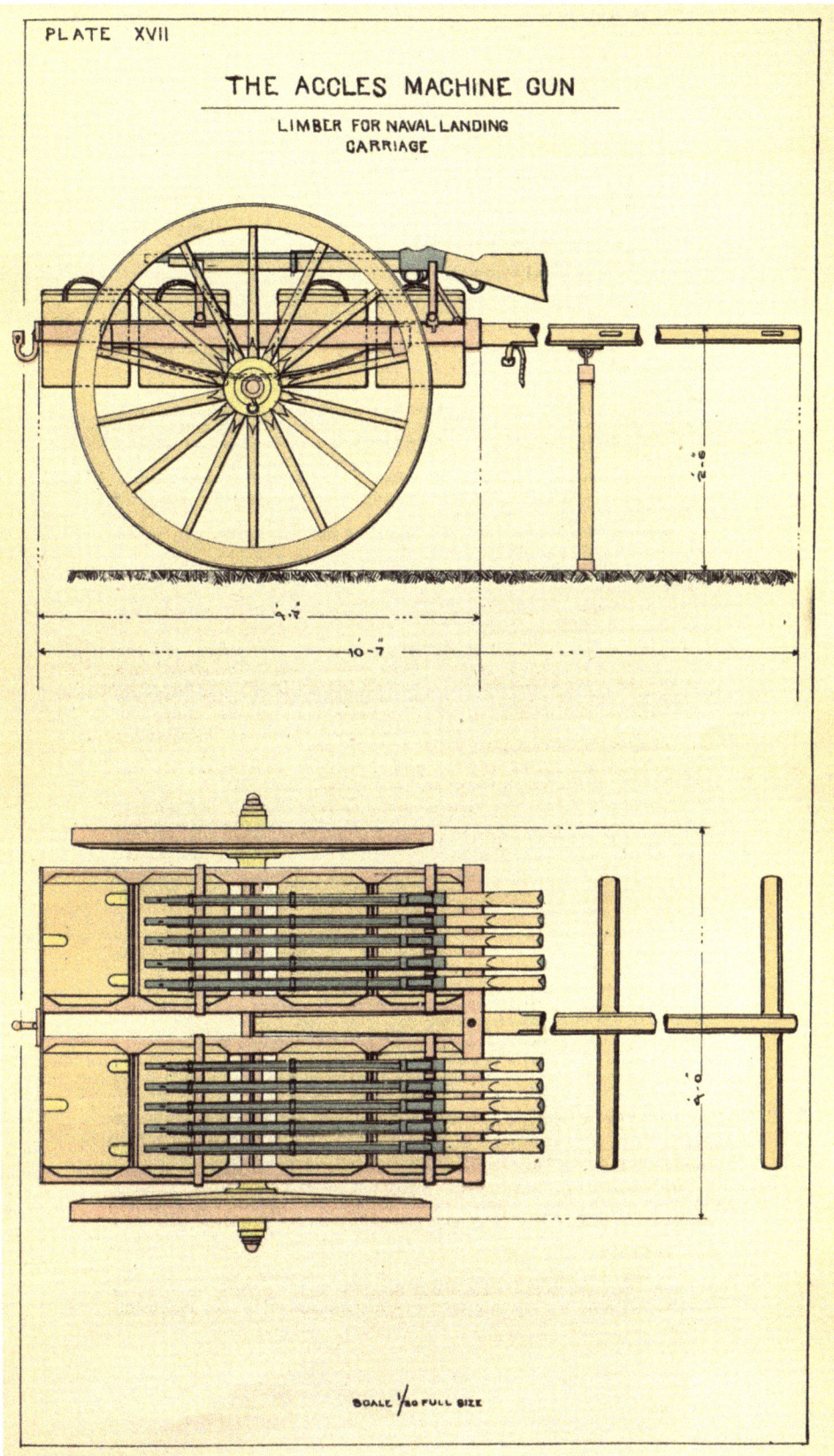

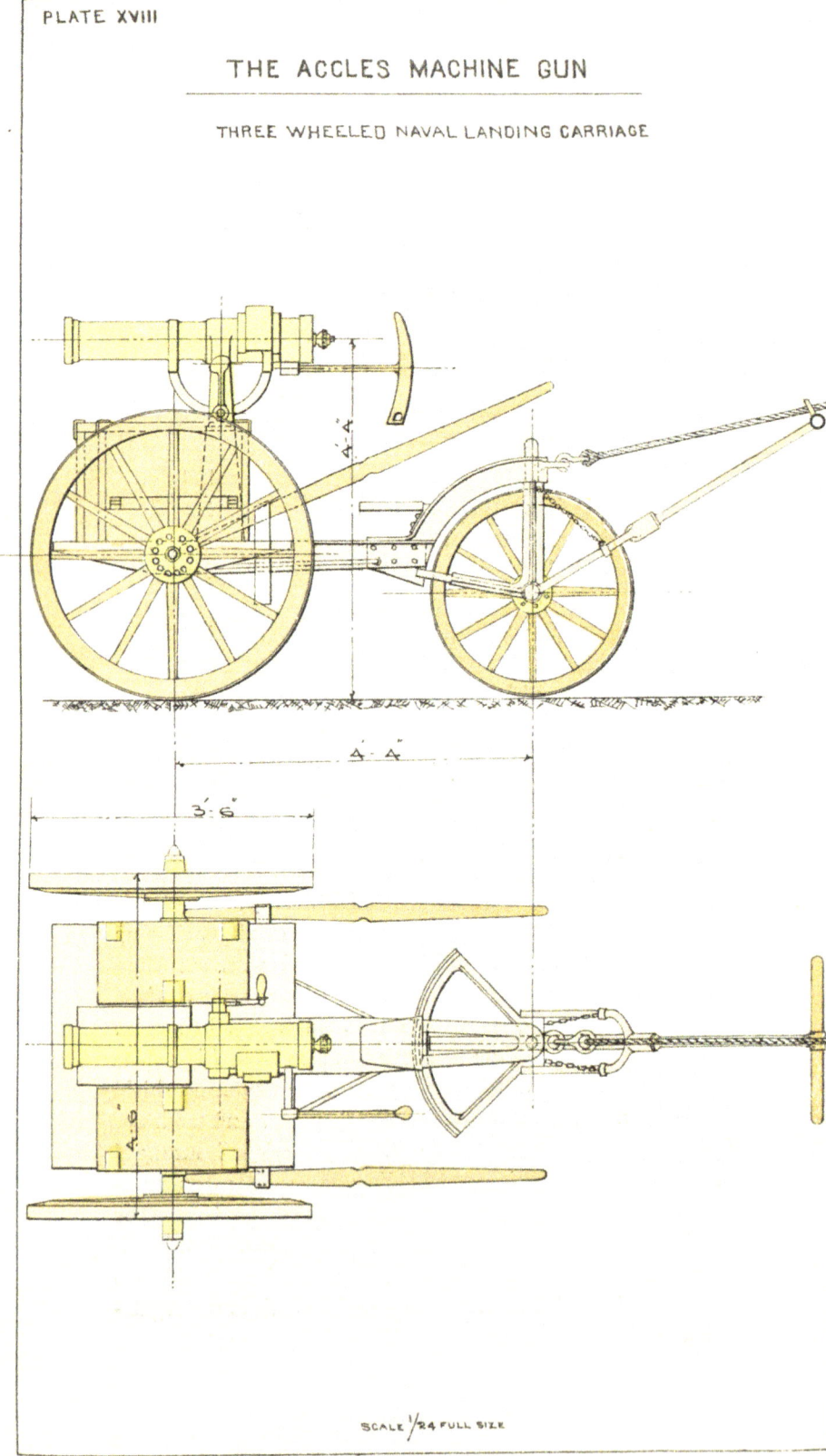

PLATE XIX

THE ACCLES MACHINE GUN
METAL LINED AMMUNITION CASE

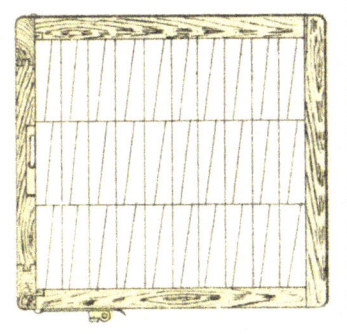

SECTION SHEWING CARTRIDGE FEED BOXES PACKED

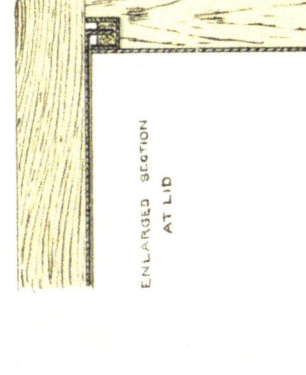

ENLARGED SECTION AT LID

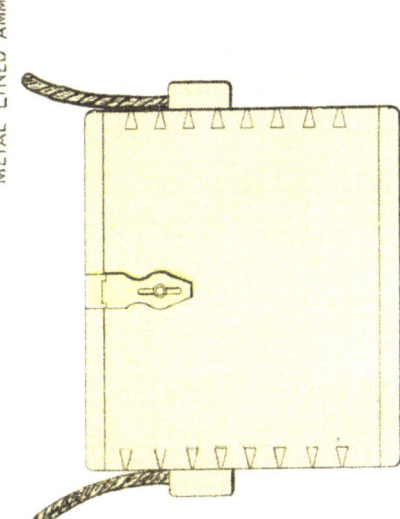

SCALE 1/7 FULL SIZE

PLATE XX

THE ACCLES MACHINE GUN

FIELD CARRIAGE

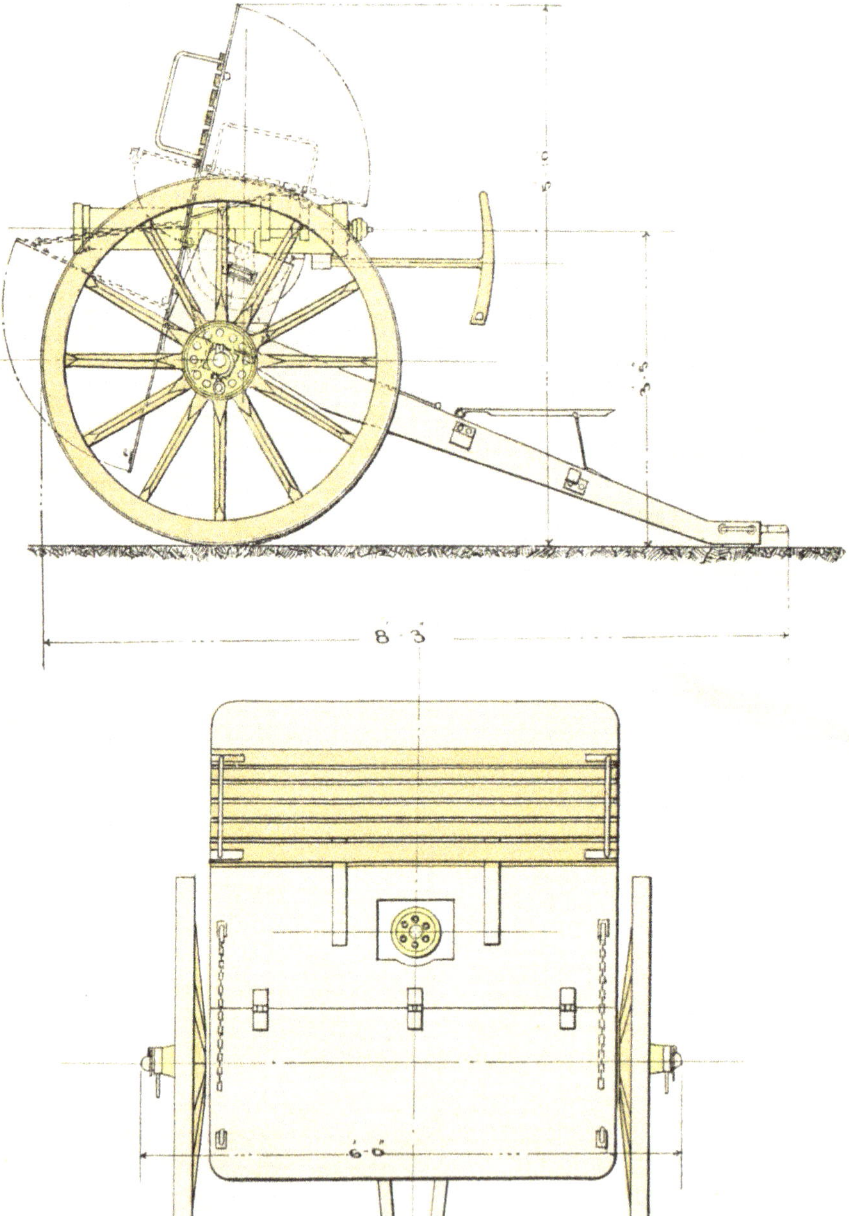

SCALE 1/24 FULL SIZE

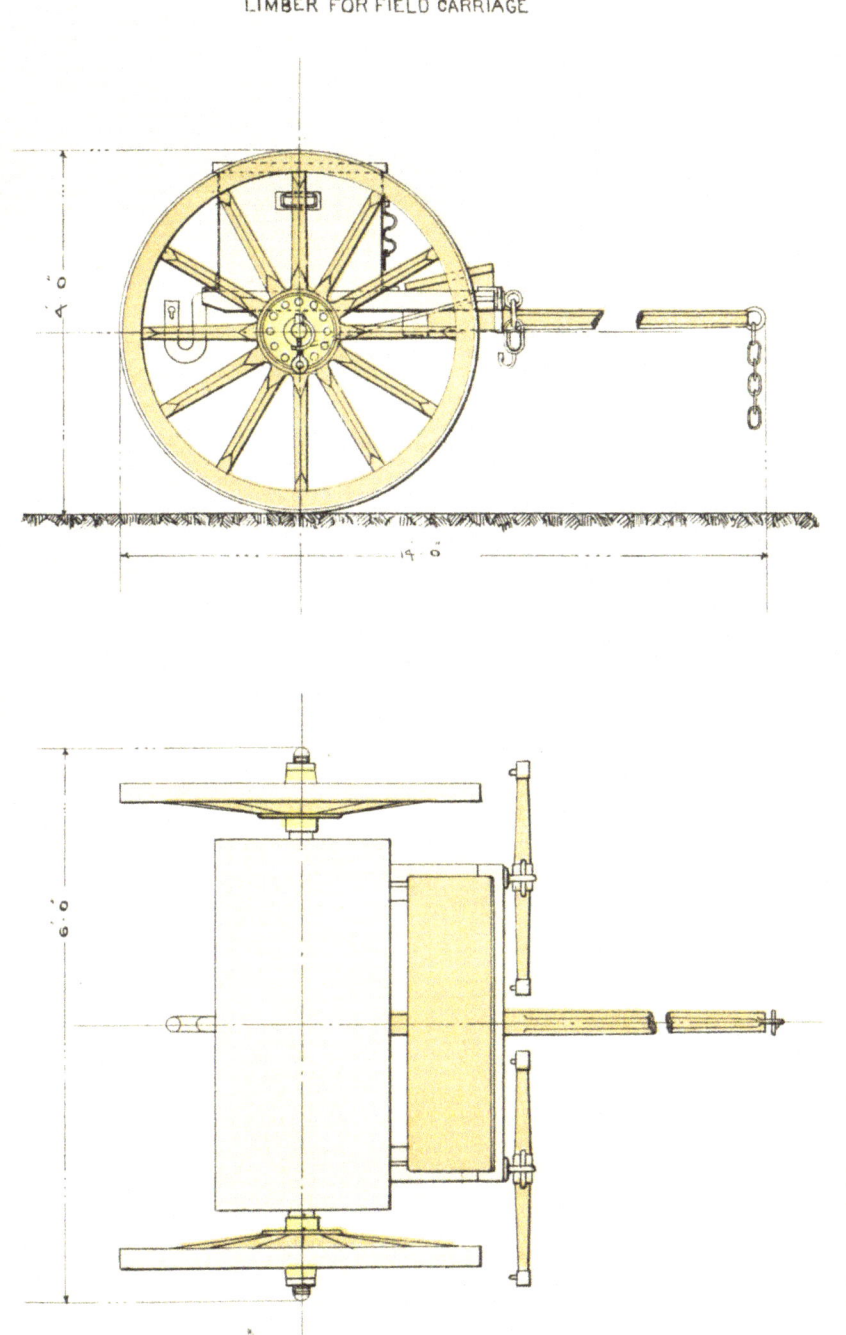

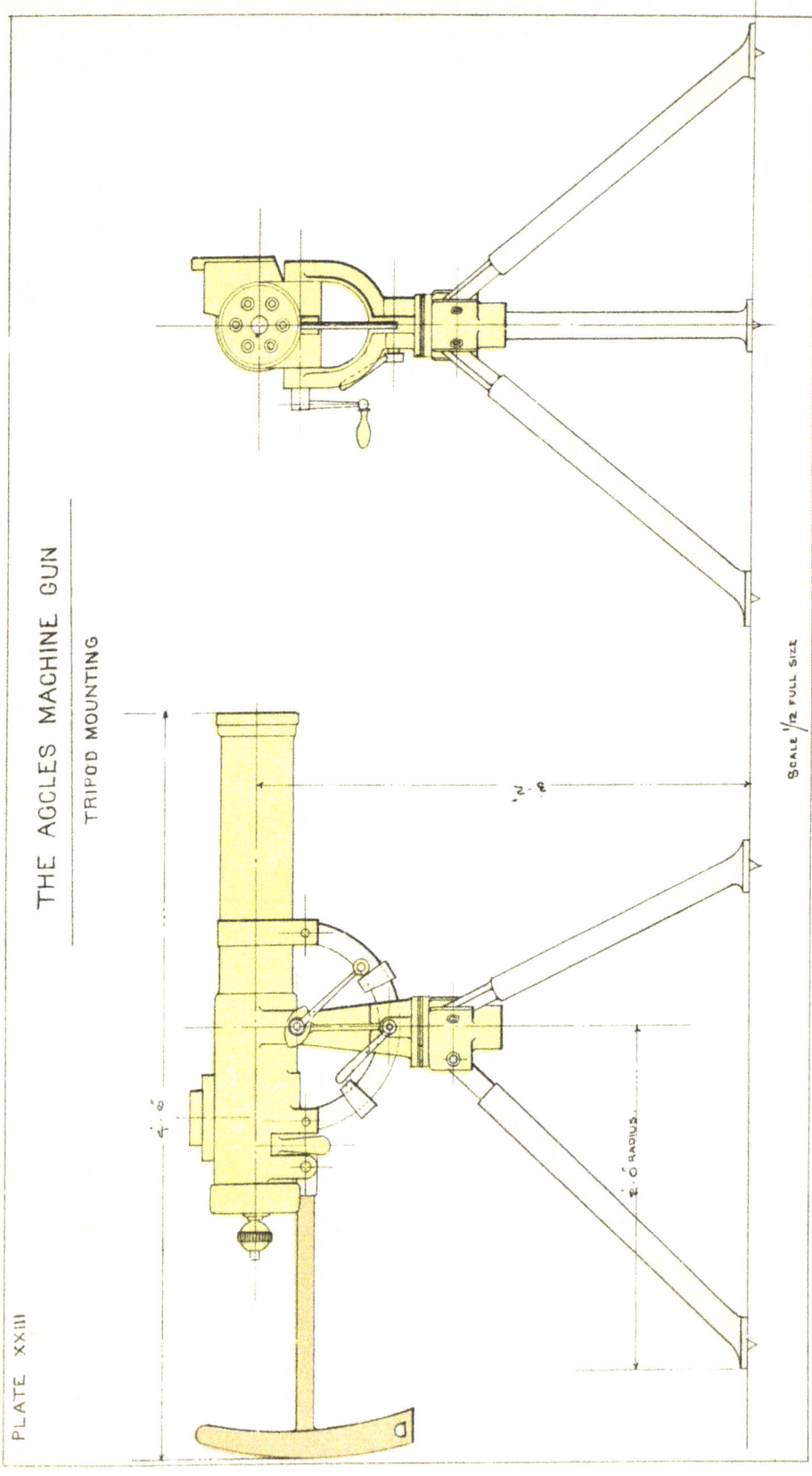

PLATE XXIV

THE ACCLES MACHINE GUN

GUN MOUNTED ON CHINESE WHEELBARROW

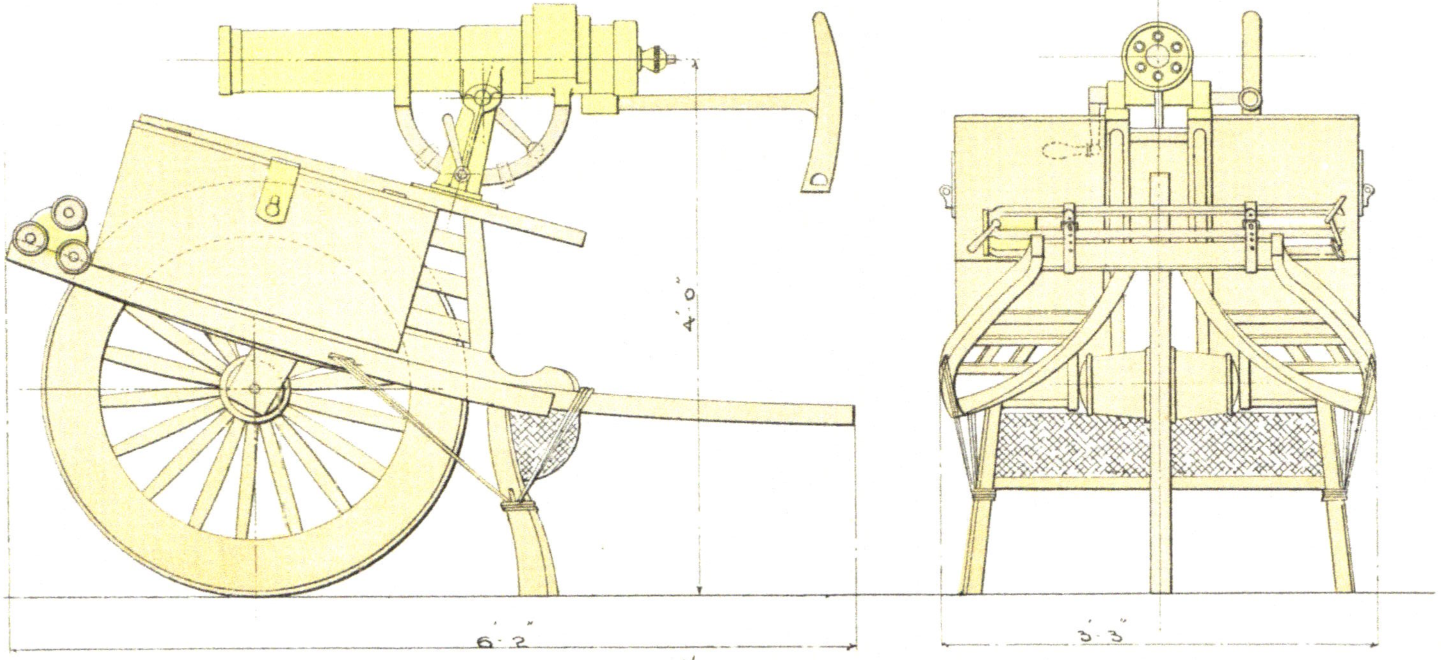

SCALE 1/8 FULL SIZE

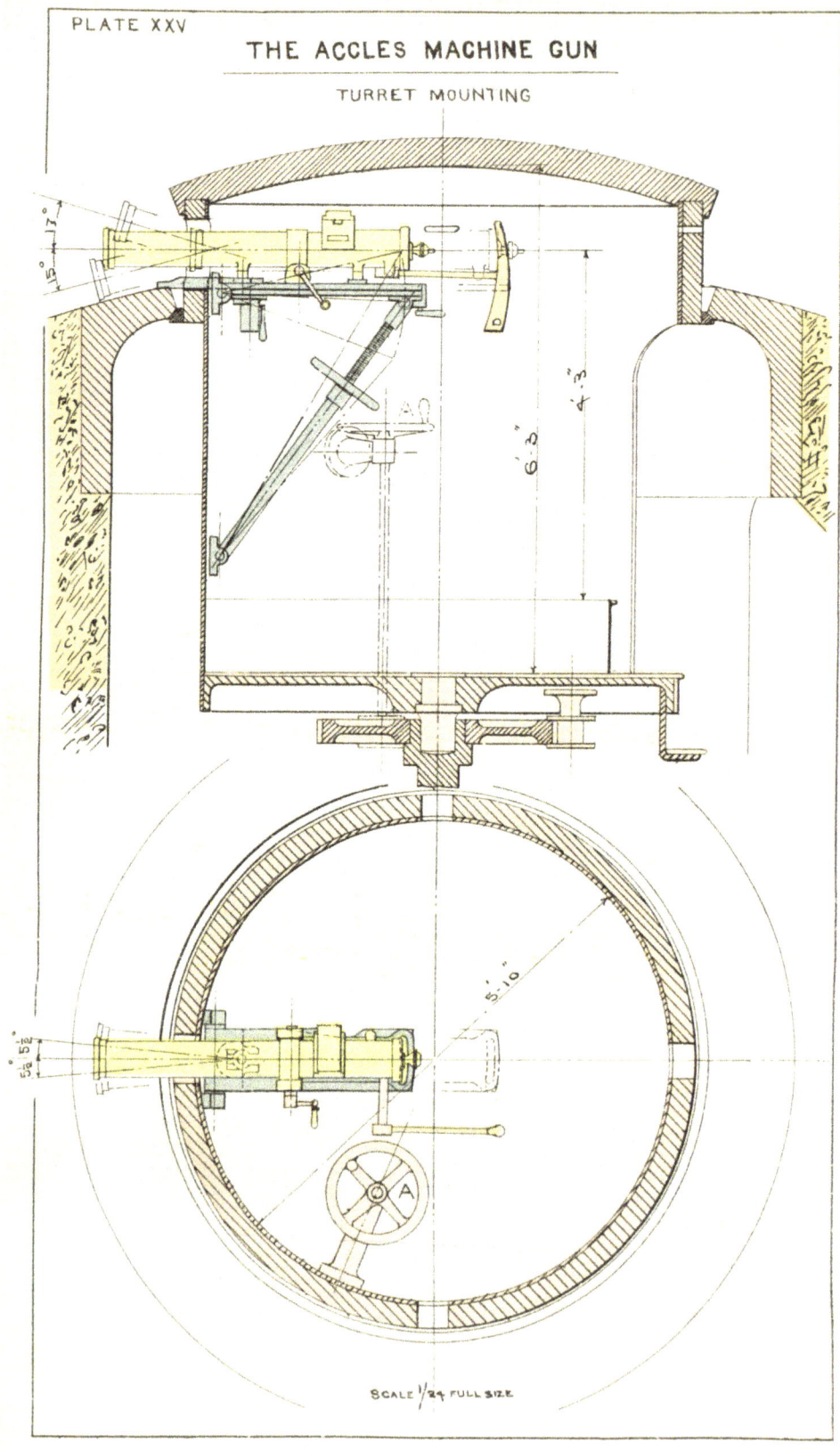

PLATE XXVI

THE ACCLES MACHINE GUN
CARTRIDGE FEED BOXES

FIG. 1.

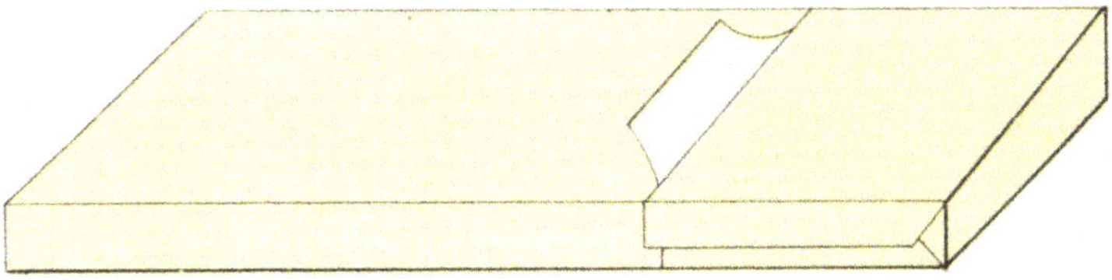

FIG. 2.

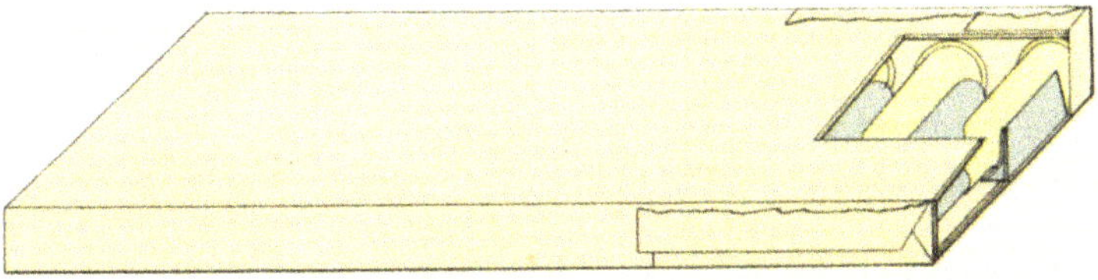

FIG. 3.

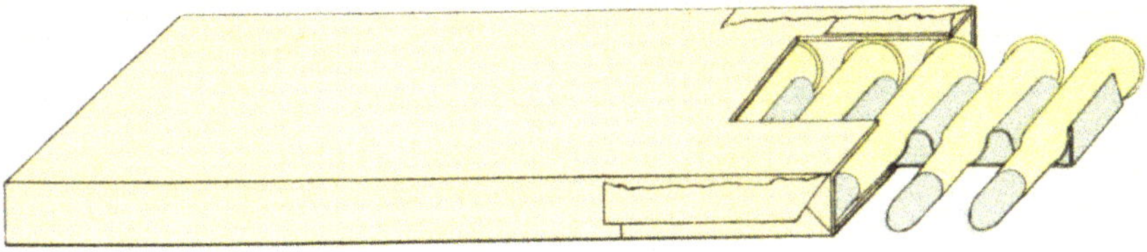

FIG. 4.

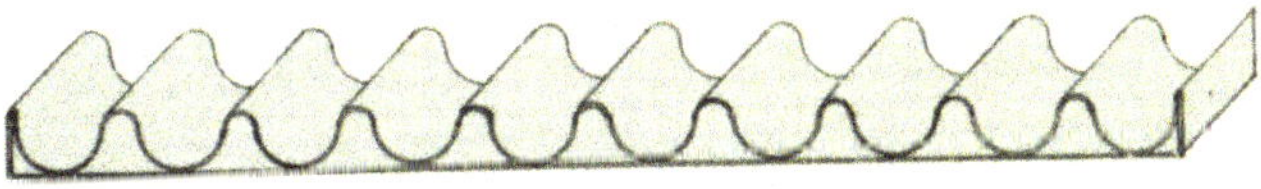

FIG. 5.

www.ingramcontent.com/pod-product-compliance
Ingram Content Group UK Ltd.
Pitfield, Milton Keynes, MK11 3LW, UK
UKHW022122230426
12048UKWH00011BA/666